Johnson & Johnson
HOSPITAL SERVICES

JANSSEN
PHARMACEUTICA

Johnson & Johnson
DENTAL PRODUCTS COMPANY

Johnson & Johnson
CARDIOVASCULAR

Codman

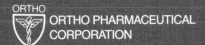
McNEIL
PHARMACEUTICAL

CRITIKON

Personal Products

ORTHO
ORTHO PHARMACEUTICAL
CORPORATION

Johnson & Johnson
ORTHOPAEDIC

A Company That Cares

A Company That Cares

Johnson & Johnson

One Hundred Year Illustrated
History of Johnson & Johnson
by Lawrence G. Foster

Copyright © 1986 Johnson & Johnson
One Johnson & Johnson Plaza
New Brunswick, New Jersey 08933

Printed in the United States of America

Library of Congress Cataloging-in-Publication Data

Foster, Lawrence G., 1925–
    A company that cares.

    1. Johnson and Johnson—History.
2. Drug trade—United States—History.
I. Johnson and Johnson
II. Title.
HD9666.9.J6F67   1986
338.7′616151′0973   86-27478
ISBN 0-9617676-1-8
ISBN 0-9617676-2-7 (soft)

We do not think of corporations as being caring, but they can be. They can also reflect many of the other emotions we reserve for people, which is not so surprising, for in the larger sense corporations are a collection of people who work together.

Over a long period, the generations of people who comprise a business organization tend to create for it a personality. On the 100th anniversary of the founding of JOHNSON & JOHNSON, this book looks at some of those people, and the events that helped to shape the Company's success as well as its personality.

JOHNSON & JOHNSON is an unusual company in many respects. Actually, it is not one, but 160 companies in fifty-five countries, each with its own mission in health care. Together they represent the largest and most diversified health care company in the world, and the only one serving all twenty-three medical specialties, from anesthesiology to urology.

Every one of the affiliates comprising this family of companies has its own identity—including its own name. All told, there are some 77,000 employees, representing virtually every culture in the world. Yet, being a part of JOHNSON & JOHNSON means having a common bond, as well as a shared sense of pride in the Company and what it represents.

That sense of pride begins with being part of a Company that has been earning the public's respect for the past century, and every day has the opportunity to have a significant impact on the health of millions of people throughout the world. It is a responsibility that is not to be taken lightly.

For most of its years JOHNSON & JOHNSON has been leading a double life—as a producer of pharmaceutical and professional products, as well as consumer products that are health related. Beginning with the introduction of JOHNSON's Baby Powder in 1894, many of the Company's consumer products have achieved worldwide popularity and acceptance. Each day gives millions of consumers the opportunity to make a choice involving JOHNSON & JOHNSON products — a choice that, if made in the Company's favor, can mean another vote of confidence.

The Company also takes justifiable pride in its past accomplishments. Beginning as it did in the infancy of modern medicine, JOHNSON & JOHNSON joined the physician in the struggle against disease and infection. It was a time when life itself was fragile, and the most modest medical advances reaped huge rewards in terms of lives saved. Probably no area of human progress has made such remarkable gains in one century as has medical science—going as it has from virtual ignorance to vast knowledge of the human body. Joining in that experience, and contributing to that progress, JOHNSON & JOHNSON went from a humble beginning to its present status.

In many respects, it has been a fascinating journey through the years, and some of the milestones along the way are touched on here. There have been countless unsung heroes in the JOHNSON & JOHNSON success story: dedicated men and women at all levels, from production line to management, who worked hard and made good things happen for the Company, and for themselves and their families.

The person most responsible for building the early JOHNSON & JOHNSON into a major international business enterprise was Robert Wood Johnson, known as "the General." He was an incurable idealist and a prodigious generator of new ideas, and he pursued each of them as though it would be his last. Many of Johnson's concepts resulted in more modern approaches to business management: he placed strong emphasis on improving human relations in the workplace, and shocked many of his fellow industrialists by building plants that adhered to his "Factories Can Be Beautiful" theme.

One of Johnson's most important concepts had an enormous influence on increasing business's responsibility to society—more

particularly, JOHNSON & JOHNSON's. He first expressed
this idea in 1935 when he declared that business had
a responsibility — he called it an obligation — to give
something back to society in return for the privileges
it enjoyed. A decade later he clearly defined what
he saw as JOHNSON & JOHNSON's commitments in a
one-page document he called the Credo. From a
pragmatic viewpoint, Johnson felt that following the
Credo was also good business. Since then the Credo
has become the cornerstone of the Company's
beliefs, and a force for binding together a highly
decentralized organization.

A̤long with its many
successes, JOHNSON & JOHNSON has also experienced
disappointment, failure and tragedy. At times when
it was severely tested, the Company's spirit and
character always prevailed.

Through the years, the one
accolade about JOHNSON & JOHNSON that keeps being
repeated is the simple but meaningful statement:
"It's a good place to work." There are many reasons
for that, but perhaps the most important one is that
the Company has always been able to attract quality
people. This is no accident, for quality people tend to
attract other quality people. A synergy develops, and
for years this has been going on within JOHNSON &
JOHNSON — and the rest is history.

LAWRENCE G. FOSTER

The ominous thunder of Civil War battles was rumbling through the South in 1861 when 16-year-old Robert Wood Johnson left his home in the Pennsylvania countryside to become an apprentice in an apothecary in Poughkeepsie, New York. At Wood & Tittamer's on Market Street young Johnson was schooled in the art of mixing medicinal plasters by his uncle, James Wood. He was a quick learner and several years later moved on to New York City, eager to apply his new found skill to the burgeoning medical products business.

First as a salesman and then as an importer of drug products, Johnson broadened his knowledge of the business. Then in 1873 he began a stormy partnership with George Seabury, who, like Johnson, was both forceful and stubborn. Under the name Seabury & Johnson the business flourished, as did their squabbling. The relationship became further strained when Johnson brought his two younger brothers, James and Edward Mead, into the business.

Early in 1886 the Johnson brothers decided to form their own medical products company. One day, while searching for a suitable factory, James was riding a westbound Pennsylvania Railroad train in New Jersey. When it slowed to cross the Raritan River at New Brunswick, he looked out the window and spied a "To Let" sign on a four-story red brick building nestled among a cluster of factories along the river bank. He ended up renting the fourth floor of what had been a wallpaper factory, and this would soon become the first home of JOHNSON & JOHNSON.

The three brothers brought a combination of skills to the business. James was adept at designing and building new production machinery. Mead, as he was known, was good at sales and advertising. Robert was the entrepreneur, and once he unraveled his legal ties to George Seabury he became the driving force behind the new firm. He was also the one with the capital that was needed to get the business started.

While the selection of New Brunswick as the home of JOHNSON & JOHNSON had been pure chance, it was nonetheless an excellent choice. Located midway between New York and Philadelphia, the city was served by rail, waterway and the main coach roads. It became a thriving commercial center, which belied its sleepy, small-town appearance.

The Raritan River offered easy access to the sea, which had appealed to the Dutch settlers when they arrived in 1730. Later a charter was granted and named for the House of Brunswick, then occupying the throne of England. During the Revolutionary War Alexander Hamilton held off the British in New Brunswick while George Washington regrouped his forces. The armies of Cornwallis and Howe later camped here, on what was to become the campus of Rutgers University.

When the Delaware and Raritan Canal opened in 1834 its northern terminus was at New Brunswick, making the city one of the busiest inland ports in America. Dozens of small, diverse industries sprang up, among them a hosiery mill, a maker of fruit jars, three rubber companies turning out footwear, and a needle factory. The Johnson brothers' firm joined them, prepared to produce an array of medicated plasters and other health care products.

The city became a magnet for large numbers of factory workers, many of them immigrants from Germany, Ireland and Hungary. Hard-working and devoted to job and family, they clustered in neighborhoods where they kept their cultural traditions alive. Travelers and tradesmen descended on the city in waves, keeping business flourishing at hotels and some fifty saloons. The gallery of the popular Opera House, a favorite stage for performers bound for New York, was always filled with raucous visitors. But despite this hubbub, New Brunswick leaned toward a serenity influenced in part by the growing college campus in its midst. It was chartered as Queen's College in 1766 by authority of King George III and opened in New Brunswick in 1771. A half century later it was renamed for Colonel Henry Rutgers, who contributed $5,000 to the institution and gained a measure of immortality. It was across from the ivy-clad Rutgers campus that the Johnson brothers established their business.

The art of making medicinal plasters was the focus of Robert Johnson's early training. From the dawn of civilization people had sought new methods of treating injuries and ailments. One early technique was to apply to the skin the juices and gums of roots, herbs, plants and trees, and animal substances as well. All were found to contain healing medicants that were absorbed through the pores. New experimentation continued through all cultures: the Chinese tried opium and elephant fat, the Egyptians slime from the Nile, the Hindus arsenic and astringent herbs, the Greeks poppy juice and mustard seed.

At the same time, new methods were developed for keeping the medications in closer contact with the skin for prolonged periods. This led to the evolution of plasters containing healants. The Pueblo Indians made plasters spread on skins of animals, leaves and flexible barks. The early colonists learned these techniques from the various American Indian tribes and added improvements of their own. Primitive as it was, the concept proved to be sound. Many of the wonder drugs developed in later years came from plants first brought to the attention of scientists because of some use by an earlier society.

The methods of introducing healants into the body were varied and none gained more sustained support than the skin plaster. Robert's early efforts at making plasters at Wood & Tittamer, like those of all who toiled at the art, were back-breaking and frustrating. He labored in the workroom at the drugstore with an iron heated over a spirit lamp, trying to mold crude rubber into a pliable mass that could be shaped in the form of a medicated plaster.

In later years he looked back on these early experiences: "Probably no other branch of the pharmaceutical art has been the occasion of so much toil, anxiety, failure and discouragement before any measure of success was met."

Reflecting on the frustrations, he added, "…expressive expletives could not be restrained."

Later, when he went to New York, Johnson became imbued with the idea of making pharmacopoeial plasters in rubber combination, which was then considered a major advance. He explained how he went about it: "Not knowing the secrets of patent plasters and of grinding rubber, we commenced upon the benzine process. With a barrel of benzine, a mixing pot, and a brush, we worked upon this method for two years only to find, after great loss, that many of the medicaments required by the pharmacopoeia were not compatible with rubber dissolved in a solvent, and that the products were not fitted for therapeutic use and commercially were worthless.

"Then commenced the struggle to combine rubber with the gums and drugs without a solvent. Some of the difficulties were to obtain sufficient power and proper machinery to grind the rubber, and then to get it plastic and adhesive. Each combination of drug presented new problems. When the mechanical troubles were overcome, decomposition would take place, and when stability was reached, there was no therapeutic action."

The practice of medicine was still in its primitive stages. Scientific knowledge of the body's functions was woefully limited. With sardonic humor, the distinguished physician Oliver Wendell Holmes described the sobering realities of nineteenth century medicine: "I firmly believe that if the whole *materia medica*, as now used, could be sunk to the bottom of the sea, it would be all the better for mankind — and all the worse for fishes."

Yet, in his limited area, young Johnson was contributing to the shallow reservoir of medical knowledge. In forming his own business he could put what he had learned to work.

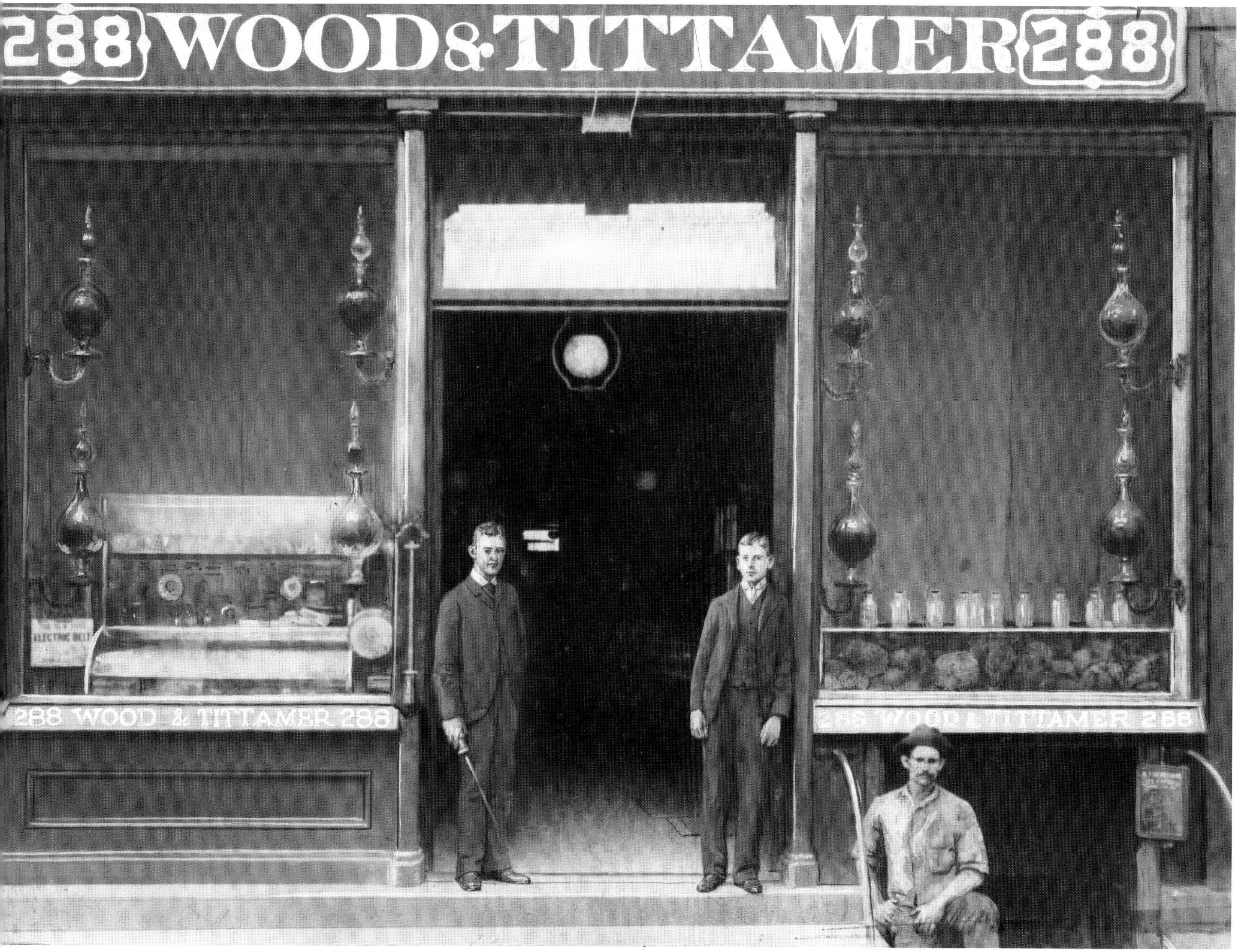

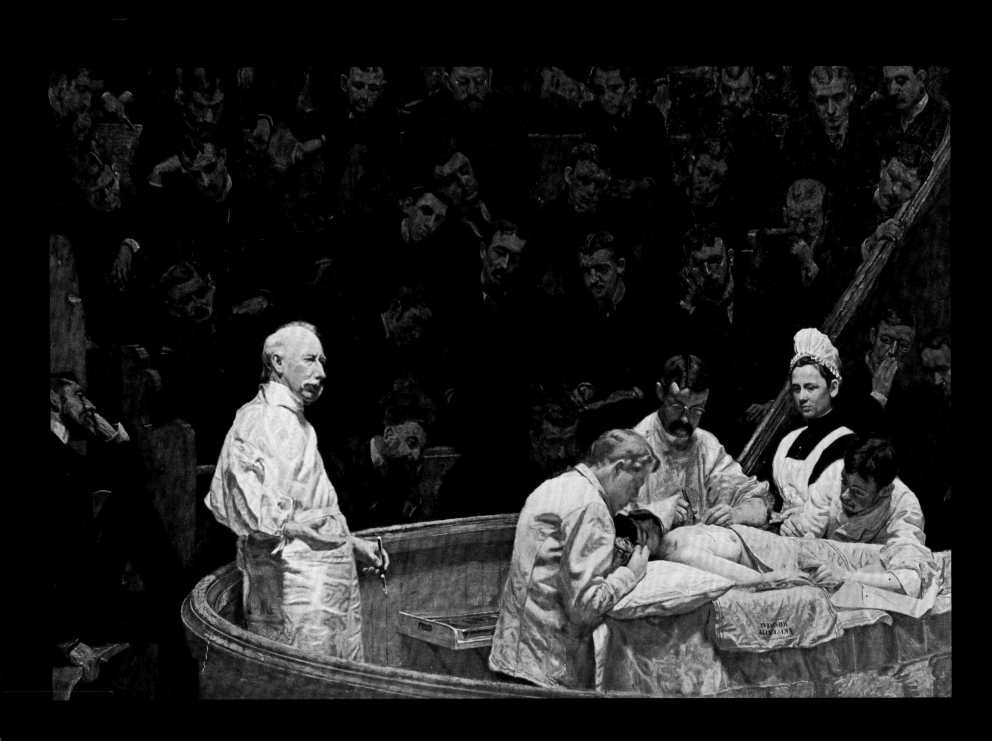

Sir Joseph Lister

Surgery in the mid-1800s was still considered nothing short of a dreadful gamble. As Sir James Simpson, a noted Edinburgh physician, described it: "The man laid on the operating table in one of our surgical hospitals is exposed to more chances of death than was the English soldier on the fields of Waterloo."

In Ancient Greece the physician had been an artisan, in the Middle Ages a priest, and in the Renaissance he became a doctor. Now, as the Twentieth Century approached, many doctors were becoming hospital physicians.

The progress of hospital care in the United States was well behind that of Europe, where all of the art of healing was at least a generation advanced. The original concept of hospitals in colonial America was to provide a place for medical care of the indigent and others who could not be properly cared for at home. Most hospitals were private institutions, known as voluntary hospitals and managed by trustees or governors, much the same as orphanages. They were staffed by physicians and surgeons who donated their services in return for access to interesting cases for teaching and research. Home was the place where infants were born, the sick were cared for and most people died.

Aversion to hospitals began to break down when physicians started using them for private patients. The patients, in turn, began to realize that many illnesses could be treated more effectively in hospitals than at home. But successful surgery, which logically could be performed better in a hospital, still eluded the medical profession principally because sterilization had not yet been discovered. The mortality rate for surgical patients was shockingly high, and no one was sure why.

As the 1800s wore on, the science of bacteriology began its telling and dramatic role in patient survival. The credit for that breakthrough belonged to Joseph P. Lister, the English surgeon who founded modern antiseptic surgery when he proved Louis Pasteur's theory that bacteria cause infection. Until that time virtually all of medicine was oblivious to the relationship between bacteria, infection and death following surgery.

Strong views were expressed by many distinguished surgeons both in support and condemnation of Lister's theory. The fact that this revelation took so long to be accepted was, in part, due to the skepticism, intransigence and indifference that greeted many innovations during that dogma-choked period in medical history. And in no instance was this resistance stronger than it was to Lister's "invisible germ" theory. He put his antisepsis theory to its first real test when he sprayed an operating room with choking clouds of carbolic acid that billowed forth from a strange looking device. The pungent mist disinfected the surrounding air, and also threatened to asphyxiate surgeons, nurses and patients alike. But most important, it worked.

Robert Johnson was among the early believers in Lister's theories about the presence of airborne germs, having heard the eminent surgeon speak at a medical conference in Philadelphia during the nation's 1876 centennial celebration. He came away impressed, and with visions of a whole new business emerging from the manufacture of antiseptic surgical dressings. Johnson had the right idea, but it wasn't until ten years later that his dream was realized. Antiseptic surgical dressings were among JOHNSON & JOHNSON's first products. Though this was a major advance in medical care, the ultimate goal of achieving perfectly sterile dressings was still out of reach.

Newspaper reports of the size of JOHNSON & JOHNSON's initial work force were overly optimistic, for when the Company commenced production in March of 1886 there were just 14 factory workers. The Company was incorporated on October 28, 1887, with an authorized capital stock of $100,000. Of this, forty percent was held by Robert and thirty percent each by James and Mead. On February 21, 1888, Robert was elected president, Mead became secretary and James was made general manager of manufacturing. By now the work force had increased to 125 and the factory area had spread to 35,000 square feet in two buildings adjoining the original loft.

It was a good time to start a new business. The demeanor of the country, depressed by the agonizing Civil War, was now decidedly upbeat. This change of national attitude coincided with an explosion of new ideas for products to meet the needs and whims of a population eager to buy them. At the very top of the priority list were those products that promoted better health. People were anxious to feel better and the health of the nation, due to neglect and ignorance, was truly in need of improve-

ment. But now the quiet revolution taking place in medicine was beginning to manifest itself in ways not even dreamed of a short time earlier. Through the early months of 1887 the Johnsons worked diligently on the Company's first catalog and price list. The thirty-two pages were crammed with an array of products sold in the outlands of the country by "travelers," many of whom had acquired medical degrees but were finding it difficult to establish a practice.

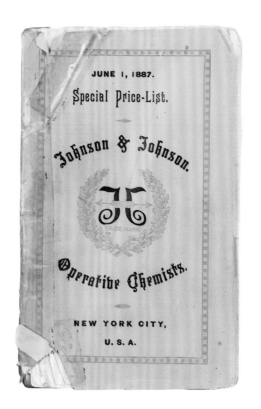

Some fourteen pages of the first catalog were devoted to an assortment of medicated plasters using Johnson's new India rubber base formula. The medicants he used in plasters included many of the formulas contained in the *U.S. Pharmacopoeia,* such as zinc oxide, opium, hemlock, quinine, pitch, burgundy, belladonna and mustard. Despite the variety, the two most popular were plasters made from the lowly mustard seed and the belladonna plant, and each had its own therapeutic action.

Mustard plasters generated considerable heat, acting as a counter-irritant and drawing blood to the injured area of the body. Belladonna plasters, made from the root extract of a plant traced to ancient Greece, acted on the body in a different way. The belladonna was combined with boracic acid, which caused the fatty tissues of the skin to hasten absorption of the belladonna into the body. Increasingly extravagant claims were made for belladonna's curative powers. Its therapeutic

uses ranged from bronchitis, headaches, and neuralgia, to spasms, cramps, spasmodic asthma, whooping cough, hiccoughs, and incontinence and herpes. The list was endless and, not surprisingly, belladonna plasters sold very well.

"Plasters should not only be mechanically perfect," Robert Johnson said of his products, "but above all they must be therapeutic agents, they must do good, and they must help us to alleviate pain and disease."

Next in the catalog came a variety of wound dressings that had been treated to make them antiseptic. They included some made from tarred jute, an East Indian fibrous plant used to make sacking material; and others made from oakum, a form of hemp also used to caulk seams and for packing

joints in construction work. Then came the carbolated dressings, listed as having been prepared "according to Lister's formula." Linton Moist Dressings were made from cotton gauze, a new material for this purpose. Packed in hermetically sealed jars, they were impregnated with a ten percent solution of iodoform, commonly referred to as "the skunk of surgery." The smell was overpowering, but it was a small price to pay in the battle against germs.

Robert Johnson, then forty-one, was a tall, stout man, with black hair and a generous moustache. He had large, deep brown eyes that seemed to rivet his subjects in place during discussions. Though he had a subdued sense of humor, his laughter and his arguments were always accompanied by a roll of his head, which some said was a family trait. He soon became a familiar figure in New Brunswick, taking frequent strolls "up the avenue," as he put it, with long assertive strides. On one such stroll he stopped at the Opera House Pharmacy and met its proprietor, Fred B. Kilmer. This chance meeting brought together two markedly different individuals who were destined to become bound together for the rest of their lives by their deep convictions about the need to improve medical care.

In appearance and demeanor, mild-mannered Fred "Doc" Kilmer gave no hint of the determination that constantly churned within him. Close to frail in appearance, and with a thin, elongated face accentuated by a goatee tapered to a point, Kilmer had the look of perpetual melancholy. Actually, he had an engaging personality and a ready wit, in addition to being a very astute pharmacist. That year he was serving as president of the New Jersey

Fred B. Kilmer

since 1879, having received his training at the New York College of Pharmacy and apprenticing in several states before settling in New Jersey. His early schooling was at Wyoming Seminary in Pennsylvania, which Robert Johnson had also attended earlier. A frequent customer at the pharmacy was Thomas Alva Edison, who bought supplies to use in his experimental laboratories at Menlo Park some five miles away. Kilmer sold Edison some of the carbon he used in developing the first practical incandescent lamp. On his visits Edison would go behind the prescription counter to watch Kilmer perform percolation and distillation and the other functions of pharmacy. "At my suggestion he purchased a *U.S. Dispensatory* in order to become acquainted with the nature of certain drugs and chemicals," Kilmer recalled. And on evenings when Mrs. Edison would manage to drag her husband to the opera they would first stop in Kilmer's pharmacy so she could, as Kilmer wrote, "help to spruce up the unconventional inventor and remove traces of his hurriedly prepared toilet."

Over time, Kilmer and Edison became fast friends, sharing an interest in many areas of scientific research. Kilmer, through his training as a pharmacist, devel-

oped a probing curiosity and considerable knowledge about the cultivation of plants for medicinal purposes. In the display window of his drugstore, he assembled a map showing where certain plants were grown and describing how they were used in medicine. Edison was intrigued by the display, as was Johnson, and both would spend long periods at the window of the Opera House Pharmacy studying Kilmer's elaborate display.

In one of his many visits to Kilmer's pharmacy, Johnson began discussing the teachings of Lister. Kilmer, too, was a believer, and lamented the fact that more physicians weren't practicing the basic rules of asepsis. Together they devised a plan. Kilmer would begin corresponding with a group of well-known American physicians and surgeons who were sympathetic to Lister, and learn more about their experiences with the sterilization method. Meanwhile, Johnson and his associates would concentrate on improving sterile surgical dressings so they would be available when there was a greater demand for them.

Pharmaceutical Association, at the age of thirty-five. In later years TIME Magazine would refer to him as "the most revered pharmaceutical chemist in the country."

The Opera House Pharmacy had a stately look. Tall wood columns flanked the entrance and an elaborate carved frieze arched out gracefully to two huge fluted columns that framed the storefront. It had become a popular place, dispensing not only the medicants of the day but indulging in the latest fads such as fizzled soda water. Kilmer had been there

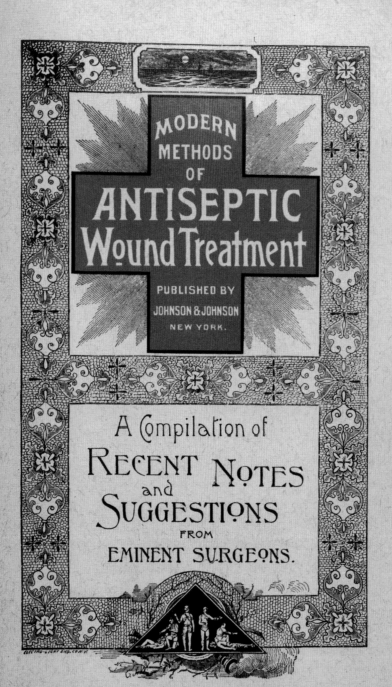

MODERN
METHODS
OF
ANTISEPTIC
Wound Treatment

PUBLISHED BY
JOHNSON & JOHNSON
NEW YORK.

A Compilation of
RECENT NOTES
and
SUGGESTIONS
FROM
EMINENT SURGEONS.

By 1888 Kilmer had gathered the views of many in the medical profession and compiled a summary, which JOHNSON & JOHNSON printed in a booklet titled: *Modern Methods of Antiseptic Wound Treatment.* In many respects it was a "how to" manual, and soon it was being proclaimed as the most authoritative treatise ever presented on the subject. The demand for it was astonishing, and within months 85,000 copies were in distribution.

In addition to being a scientific document, *Modern Methods* was also a sales catalog for Johnson's products. He had shrewdly used the back pages of the manual to display his company's growing list of products, which now included an assortment of bandages, cotton, gauzes, sutures and ligatures, iodoform sprinklers and drainage tubes.

Recognizing Kilmer's many skills, Johnson wisely asked him to join the Company as Director of Scientific Affairs. Kilmer pondered the decision for some time because of his dedication to pharmacy, but seeing the opportunity to play a larger role and to have an influence on the direction of medical science, he accepted.

The demand for *Modern Methods* continued unabated, and in time over four million copies were in distribution all over the world. One of the many distinguished surgeons who contributed to the manual was Dr. Samuel David Gross of The Philadelphia College of Medicine, the originator of various surgical techniques, including the wiring together of fractured bones. In a letter to Dr. Gross, Johnson wrote: "We are glad to be able to inform you that the antiseptic brochures have been of marked benefit to our business...." That was an understatement. The stimulating effect that the manual had on the business was remarkable. As a scientific document it was hailed as being a major contribution to the advancement of antiseptic surgery during a critical period of learning.

The educational process had begun, and while the gap separating primitive from modern surgery was still wide, the new manual was helping to bridge it. The timing was perfect, and the fact that the Johnsons also had a line of products that fitted neatly with this enlightened approach made the effort that much more rewarding. Kilmer later reflected on the role they played: "...In its very inception, while the consensus of surgical opinion was decidedly against the innovations of antiseptic and aseptic surgery, the Company boldly stepped in with new forms of surgical dressings and won out....they led the way."

Kilmer, as usual, was modest. He, too, had played a major role in bringing Lister's teachings to the attention of the medical profession. When word reached Lister about the new methods of manufacturing and sterilizing surgical dressings, he wrote asking for details. On December 28, 1891, he was sent a lengthy response outlining every step of the process. The inquiry generated a swell of pride among the employees of JOHNSON & JOHNSON. The man who discovered the techniques of sterile surgery was now interested in the further advances they had made in the art. Soon production was soaring and the work force was constantly being increased. This required expansion to various nearby buildings.

Soon the Company had acquired the technical expertise that it needed to mass produce sterile cotton and gauze dressings. In 1891 a new bacteriological laboratory was built in Highland Park, where the classic laboratory experiments conducted earlier in Germany by Robert Koch were duplicated with great care. They demonstrated the efficacy of hot air and steam in killing microorganisms, and from these experiments Kilmer developed a procedure for verifying the industrial process by using reference organism spores of *Bacillus anthracis*, an organism also favored by Koch. First he inoculated a portion of the dressing material. Then the contaminated dressing was placed in the center of the other dressings in the sterilizer load. If the steam killed the test organisms, the remaining dressings were also presumed to be sterile. Through these procedures Kilmer developed the biological indicator in industrial sterilization. He constantly sought to improve his methods to achieve his goal that " …a dressing must be more than antiseptic, it also must be free of microorganisms."

Commenting on how far they had come, Kilmer wrote: "Chemical sterilization and mechanical cleanliness are among the newer weapons that have been called to the aid of surgery. Antiseptic dressings have been made surgically clean. Antisepsis has not been abandoned, but has developed into its higher form: asepsis. Antiseptic processes have now become aseptic."

As correct as Lister had been about the need for a germ-free environment, even he had failed to grasp that the materials from which surgical dressings were then made were not satisfactory. Nor had he seen the importance of absorbency in surgical dressings. From the beginning the Johnsons saw the value of absorbency, and they determined that the correct material to use was cotton. The experiments went on endlessly to find better ways to clean, bleach and comb out cotton to produce soft, white absorbent dressings. Eventually the process would involve forty separate steps. Making the cotton and gauze antiseptic, and later sterile, was yet another challenge.

Several years after its founding the Company began packaging absorbent cotton in small quantities, wrapped in blue tissue paper and placed in blue cartons with a red cross on the label. Small amounts of cotton could be removed from the box without contaminating the remainder. In time, the blue box of cotton with the red cross would become one of the most recogniz-able products in America. Soon there were other variations of cotton. Lintine was made of a cotton fiber and came in sheets so it could be cut or torn and used in layers. Dental patients became very familiar with Cottonoid, small cylinder-shaped rolls of compressed cotton that the dentist packed in patients' mouths.

Hospitals in America in the late 1800s were just emerging as centers of medical care. The Johnsons were among the first in the medical supply field to see this trend. The original concept that hospitals were to provide medical care for indigent patients had changed and, as the advantages became evident, improvements were added. Hospital laboratories for X-ray, bacteriology and chemistry were opened in the 1880s, and as the application of asepsis began to take hold and the surgery mortality rate began dropping, more operating rooms were built in hospitals.

Many were designed with sterility in mind. Patients with communicable diseases were isolated in special pavilions, and paying patients had private rooms set apart from the indigent. Training schools for nurses were started; they added greatly to the quality of patient care but introduced another problem. Conflicts arose between trained nurses and physicians who felt their authority was being threatened.

The growing demand for the Company's innovative products pushed production to the limits, and led to further expansion of factory space that now embraced buildings right down to the river's edge. Memories of the Company's "feeble beginning," as Robert Johnson once described it, were fast fading. The nation was fighting its way back from the brink of economic disaster following the financial panic of 1893, when some 16,000 businesses went bankrupt and 600 banks failed. But somehow the medical business found itself impervious to these economic pitfalls, and by the end of 1894 employment at JOHNSON & JOHNSON had risen to 400, and manufacturing and office space occupied fourteen buildings. Factory output was up sharply, with cotton being processed at the rate of 4,000 pounds a day and plaster production at 15,000 pounds. Gauze output was now an impressive 3,500,000 yards a year. Each morning a steamship would pull alongside the dock and load a cargo stamped "JOHNSON & JOHNSON." Then it would wend its way down the Raritan and up to New York harbor, passing the new Statue of Liberty enroute to a Hudson River

pier. There the products would be transferred to distribution points for domestic and foreign markets.

What was happening at JOHNSON & JOHNSON, now employing hundreds of workers who had come to America as immigrants, was symbolic of the rising spirit and vitality sweeping the nation in the late 1800s. The country's transformation from an agrarian society to an industrialized one was rapidly occurring.

Amid these upheavals of tradition, most people clung to a belief in the American rags-to-riches dream. The Horatio Alger myth had been popularized by the likes of Andrew Carnegie and John Jacob Astor. Carnegie rose to wealth and fame from his start as a bobbin boy earning $4.80 a month in a Pittsburgh textile mill. Astor arrived on these shores with five dollars in his pocket, and became the richest man in the country. Their stories were told and retold, and they kindled hope, particularly among those who were ambitious.

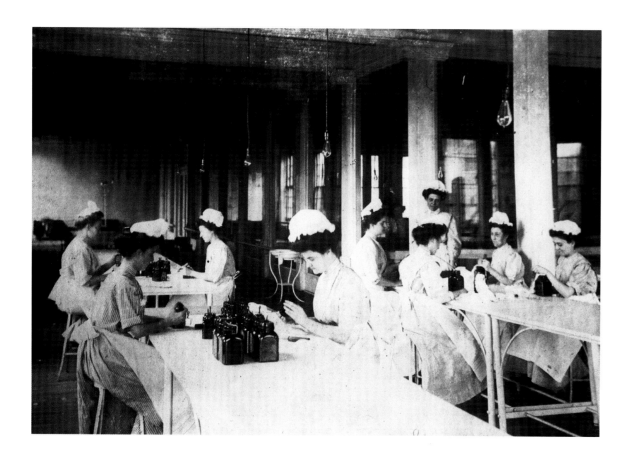

were washed and sterilized right on the premises. Women employees from the first day began wearing white nurse-type hats, and this became a tradition.

There was a constant search for new products. The concept of disposable products was relatively new. Johnson developed an ingenious one for which he obtained a patent. It was an oval-shaped sponge made of layers of absorbent cotton and coconut and manila fibers. In the center was a small capsule filled with an antiseptic. The physician was instructed to squeeze the capsule just before using the sponge, thereby releasing the antiseptic. New plasters were made with unusual formulas. A product called Canthos contained *U. S. Pharmacopeia* strength Spanish fly, best known for its aphrodisiac claims. The body fluids of these South European bluish green insects contained cantharadin, a substance that caused the skin to blister. When mixed with tars and gums it became a highly effective plaster to produce heat and enhance healing.

By now JOHNSON & JOHNSON was widely regarded as the pioneer of antiseptic and sterile surgical dressings in America. A broad array of dressings had been devised and put at the disposal of physicians who were now flocking to the practice of Listerism in growing numbers. The importance of the Company's role was not limited to products, for it had become the center of reliable information on new approaches to surgery and patient care.

As its reputation grew, so did the need for uncompromising product quality. Employees were constantly reminded that there was no such thing as "a nearly sterile product." Here Robert Johnson once again asserted himself, insisting on absolute cleanliness in the production area and venting his anger whenever he found violations. The rules of cleanliness were strict. All production employees wore uniforms or coveralls that

Very truly yours
Clara Barton

The red cross symbol, which now identified much of the Company's packaging, had become a valuable asset. So it was with great concern that discussions began in 1895 with the indomitable Clara Barton, who had publicly expressed fears about being able to protect the interests of the American Red Cross.

After her heroic acts of mercy on the Civil War battlefields, Barton had formed the American Red Cross, patterned after an international organization that had adopted the Greek red cross as its symbol. When Barton formed the American counterpart she soon became alarmed over the growing commercial use of the Red Cross symbol. When she investigated, she was dismayed to find that the Red Cross name had been adopted by a host of products. There were Red Cross Cigars, Red Cross Brandy, Red Cross Whiskey, Red Cross Playing Cards, Red Cross Washing Machines, Red Cross Stoves, Red Cross Churns, Red Cross Soap, and even Red Cross Dog Collars. Barton was flabbergasted. So in 1895 she prevailed upon the U.S. Congress to pass a bill allowing the American National Red Cross exclusive use of the symbol, with power to license its use. However, President Grover Cleveland refused to sign it into law.

The Johnsons had opposed the bill, contending that they had established the right to use the mark. This led to a series of meetings between Barton and Robert Johnson and Kilmer; finally a compromise agreement was signed on January 19, 1895. Had President Cleveland signed the congressional bill, the agreement would have allowed JOHNSON & JOHNSON to use the Red Cross symbol for the payment of one dollar. The agreement said in part: "....JOHNSON & JOHNSON now and for a long time past has been entitled at common law and otherwise to the exclusive use of the symbol of the red cross as a trademark." A decade passed before President Theodore Roosevelt signed legislation protecting the American Red Cross's use of the mark, but at the same time reserving Johnson's rights to it.

Gaining legal support for use of the Red Cross trademark came at a time when product imitation was rampant in American business. Some packages used slightly varied red crosses that were strikingly similar. Frustrated, Robert Johnson took a bold step. He had special stationery printed in color, on which were shown some of his better known products alongside pictures of the imitations. He sent these to every physician in the country with a letter that said in part: "…Red Cross Aseptic Ligatures (in the new sealed envelopes) had scarcely been placed upon the market when several imitations appeared as illustrated. While imitation is a flattering acknowledgment of the superiority of the original, we fear that where the end sought is of a commercial nature the requirements of surgery are apt

to be omitted. The cost for the original will be no greater than the other kinds."

It worked. Reports came back from many drug trade customers that they had ceased buying the imitations. In 1897 JOHNSON & JOHNSON began publishing a new monthly magazine called *Red Cross Notes*. It soon became a national forum for all types of articles and comments on developments in medicine, many of them written by physicians who recounted their experiences, both good and bad.

Red Cross Notes carried the latest bulletins on the most threatening contagious diseases: diphtheria, smallpox, typhoid, influenza, whooping

cough and tuberculosis. It promoted Company products discreetly, and no one seemed to mind because it retained its scientific integrity. "It is a matter of pride that we retain the humble attitude of the sincere student," Kilmer wrote, "and we therefore earnestly solicit correspondence." Letters from physicians came in endless waves, relating their hopes and concerns about patient care.

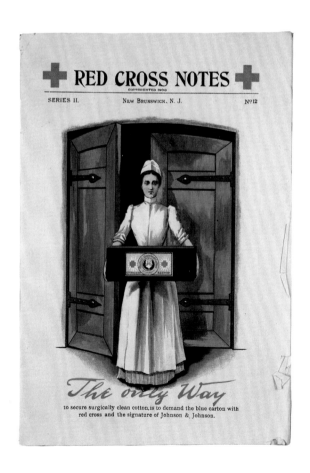

The Johnsons got into the baby powder business quite by accident. One day in 1890 a physician wrote to the Company saying that one of his patients was complaining of skin irritation from using a medicated plaster. It was Fred Kilmer who suggested sending the patient a small container of Italian talc to soothe the irritated skin. From then on a small can of talc was included with certain put-ups of plasters.

Soon customers began asking for more of the powder. This was the birth of JOHNSON's Baby Powder, destined to become one of

the best known and most enduring products in America and much of the world. When people thought of JOHNSON & JOHNSON they invariably thought of baby powder. Its delicate scent stimulated happy thoughts of childhood, and still does nearly a century later.

The sales of consumer products focused attention on the need to advertise. Shortly after the Company was formed, Robert Johnson retained the services of J. Walter Thompson, a brilliant young advertising man whom he had met several years earlier. The two became good friends, saw each other socially and often traded investment advice. Thompson had begun his career as a bookkeeper with a small agency, Carlton & Smith, and in 1878 purchased it for $500. He handled the Johnson account himself, and it was at times frustrating.

Johnson approved every ad and measured its performance according to his own yardstick. He had an instinct for what would sell, but at times he would meddle, much to the consternation of Thompson and his agency staff. The "Dear Walter" letters were often blunt. "…I return the sketch and hardly see how you can make an advertisement out of it. It needs to have a very black background in

order to throw out the white letters." That particular ad perished, but the friendship flourished, no doubt because Thompson wisely followed his cardinal rule: "Never get on stage in front of your client. No advertising can stand even the suspicion that you, not he, could have been responsible for his success."

Another new consumer product far less durable than baby powder was a bottled dental cream called Zonweiss. Translated from German it meant "white teeth." Zonweiss was vigorously promoted, and with each dozen bottles purchased druggists were offered a premium of a free clock, which came to be known as "the Zonweiss clock." The clock could be sold by druggists at any price they chose. For years there was a huge demand for Zonweiss clocks — far greater than for the dental cream. Later the dental cream was packaged in what was proclaimed to be the first squeezable toothpaste tube, but even that innovation could not keep it alive in the marketplace, and in time it disappeared, while Zonweiss clocks ticked on.

Robert Johnson worked long hours and often seemed disappointed, sometimes piqued, when others didn't do the same. Periodically he would issue a memorandum to the staff on the evils of "clockwatching," a practice which he abhorred. And since the office was small, he was able to keep personal tabs on everyone. Despite his sometimes dogmatic ways, he commanded the respect of his people and would urge them on to greater effort with one of his familiar pronouncements. A favorite was: "The worst thing that can happen to a man is to lose his courage." He would say that time and again, making believers out of doubters. When he approved a project he often would bellow: "It's a go!" It became a familiar rallying cry around the office and factory: "R.W. says it's a go!" Another was "Keep the wheels moving and everybody busy!"

His enthusiasm was widely admired, and once it was suggested that he run for mayor of

New Brunswick. He was asked if his policies would be for the good of the party, which was Republican. Johnson replied that if elected he would discharge all useless officials, cut appropriations, lower taxes, refund the debt at lower interest rates, cancel all unfair contracts and buy supplies and hire labor in the best market he could find. They decided he wouldn't make a good candidate, after all.

Since Johnson involved himself in every facet of the business, his influence was felt everywhere. He could quote precise sales figures "up to Saturday night," as he put it. And when he said orders on a particular day were light, he knew that as fact because he had personally presided over the opening of the Company mail, as he did every morning. It became a daily ritual. He would gather a group of other executives in the mail room and together they would open every letter. He paid close attention to complaints, and they often received personal replies from him. Writing letters to physicians was another of his daily chores, and this personal touch helped to make many of them lifetime customers.

Communicating with the sales force, or "travelers" as they were known, was primarily the duty of Mead Johnson. Careful attention was paid to the sales materials provided them, so that when they called on customers the correct impression would be left. As the business grew, Mead hired more travelers, giving preference to those who had been trained as physicians. They were paid $100 a month and had to cover huge territories, such as all of New England. They traveled constantly, by rail, stage and horseback, and called on wholesale and retail druggists as well as leading physicians and major hospitals.

At the time, $100 a month was considered a good salary, which Robert Johnson frequently reminded his people of in discreet ways. "It will be necessary for you to get in some hard 'licks' in order to make your work pay," he wrote one traveler. His own salary was low in the early years, and finally rose to $800 a month in the early 1890s, while James and Mead were increased to $400 a month. Gradually the Johnsons brought in additional management, but were careful in the caliber of people they hired as well as their work habits.

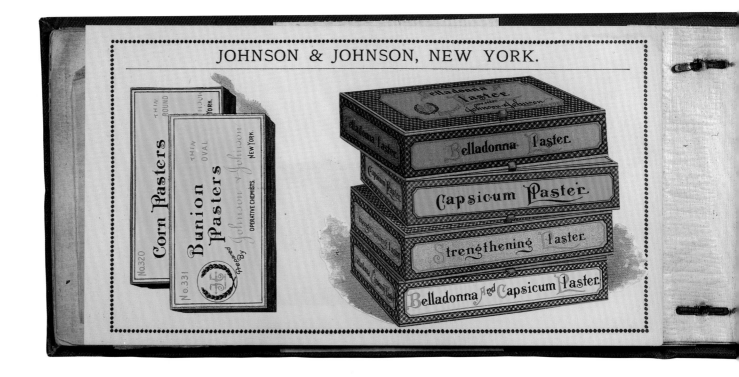

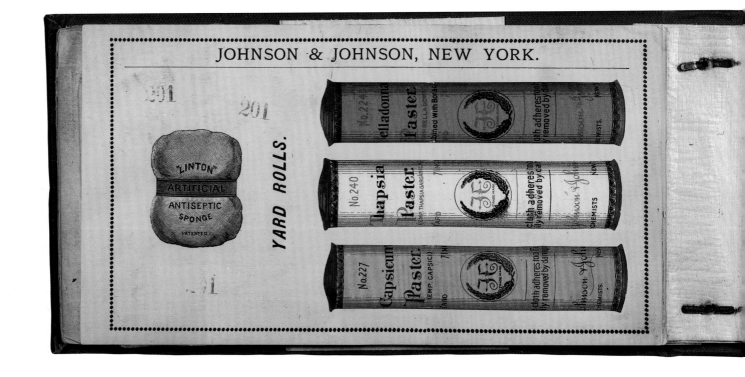

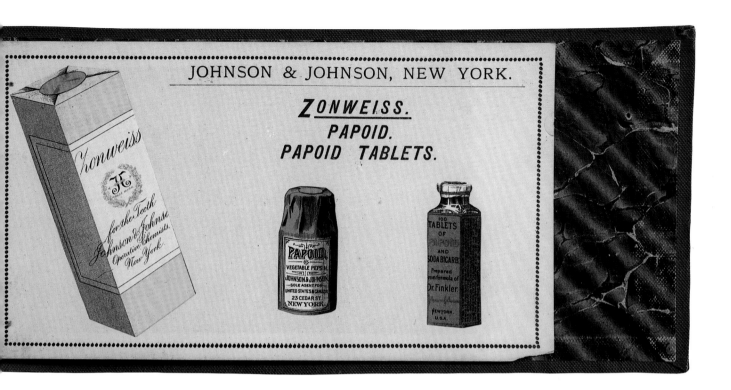

JOHNSON & JOHNSON, NEW YORK.

ZONWEISS.
PAPOID.
PAPOID TABLETS.

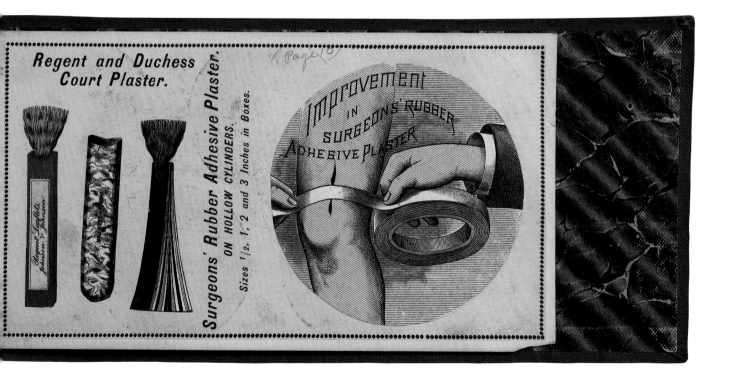

Regent and Duchess
Court Plaster.

Surgeons' Rubber Adhesive Plaster.
ON HOLLOW CYLINDERS.

Sizes 1/2, 1, 2 and 3 Inches in Boxes.

When promoting S. H. Black to a sales management position, Robert Johnson reminded him in a letter: "What we want is reliability and close attention to details… someone who, in taking charge, does not make men work more than he performs." Black learned well, and later left to form his own company, Bauer & Black, which became a fierce competitor.

When travelers visited physicians they would often get into discussions about new products. If these ideas materialized the product was often named for them: Dr. Kubin's Antiseptic Vaccination Shield; Dr. Grosvenor's Bellcapsic Porous Plaster; Dr. Simpson's Intranasal Tampon; Dr. Simpson's Maternity Packet and Dr. Don's Corn and Bunion Shields.

Expansion to overseas markets came rapidly. Agreements were signed for exclusive selling rights to Thomas Leeming in Canada, and Thomas Gilmour in England, and agents were added in Australia and New Zealand. Mead also took charge of the foreign travelers and agents, constantly urging them to be especially tactful with the leading physicians. He wrote Gilmour: "…by treating these chappies right they will do more disinterested advertising for you than the exhibit will."

Fred B. Kilmer and Alexander R. Lewis

In search of relief from a host of ailments, countless Americans were succumbing to the persuasions of wily peddlers of so-called "patent" medicines, those that could be bought without a prescription. They were dispensed by an army of charlatans from the back of buckboard wagons in rural areas, and by equally fast-talking con artists in the cities. Some of the "remedies" were homemade brews laced with alcohol, and offered a temporary lift but no real medicinal value. Other "patent" medicines were quite legitimate.

The Johnsons had been corresponding regularly with the originators of a new product called Coca-Cola that was introduced in Atlanta in 1886. A pharmacist there, John Styth Pemberton, had first experimented with a syrup derived from the coca plant and cola nuts by mixing batches of it in a brass pot in his backyard. He took a jug of the syrup to Jacobs' Pharmacy, where it was combined with carbonated water and sold for five cents a drink. After several years of sluggish sales the business was sold in 1893 to Asa G. Candler, a wholesale and retail druggist in Atlanta. Candler formed the Coca-Cola Company and began broad scale advertising of the "exhilarating" and "invigorating" drink with tonic properties.

It was the "tonic" potential that intrigued the Johnsons. Kilmer called the non-addictive stimulant an "excitant of intellect and imagination." In 1894 JOHNSON & JOHNSON introduced the first of their "kola" prepara-tions, which, among other things, was recommended for the relief of nausea, to regulate the pulse, and increase stamina and endurance. If those claims weren't appealing, it also was supposed to sober drunks. Wary of being classified with the notorious dispensers of "patent"

medicines, the Johnsons decided to restrict the sale of the kola products to their regular drug outlets, and for good measure had them approved by the American Medical Association. The best known and most popular was Vino Kolafra, or "wine of kola." This concoction contained liberal quantities of inexpensive sherry, along with the extract from the kola nuts. Sales of Vino Kolafra turned out to be not nearly so stimulating as the product itself was to those making it at the factory. When workers began sampling the sherry in ever larger quantities, the product was promptly discontinued.

Far more serious attention was being given by the Company to experiments with the

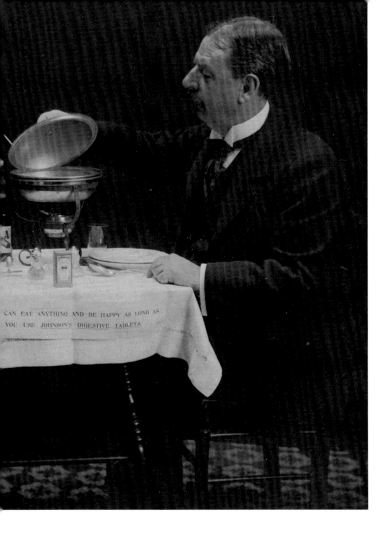

parture from JOHNSON & JOHNSON so he could strike out on his own. He sold his stock in the Company to Robert, and the friendly settlement included his taking over a small subsidiary, American Ferment Company, which had been acquired to expand the development of papain products. One of these products, Cartoid, was formulated to help infants digest cow's milk. Johnson had become very interested in infant nutrition, an area which until then had received scant attention from the medical profession.

Moving to American Ferment's tiny facility in Jersey City, Mead began planning ways to expand his business. He added several pharmaceuticals and later changed the firm name to Mead Johnson & Company. In 1915 he moved his company to Evansville, Indiana, where it became a highly successful business with infant formula its major product.

Carica papaya fruit of the papaw tree, which grew wild in Central America. The papaya's milky fluid acted on food so similarly to human gastric juices that it was considered the perfect cure for the stomach ailment dyspepsia, or indigestion, then called America's "national disease."

The first of the papaya products marketed by the Johnsons was called Papoid, which had originally been researched and developed by a German firm. Papoid carried the claim of being able to "reduce any food known to man to a soluble condition." It was first introduced in liquid form, and later as a gelatin-coated pill called Dr. Finkler's Papain. Essence of Carikola was a combination of papaya and kola, and promoted as both a digestive aid and a stimulant.

The vegetable pepsin products were of particular interest to Mead Johnson. Determined to learn more, he went to the West Indies and there found the natives using the milky juice to soften tough meat, remove stains from their clothing and blemishes from their skin.

By 1897 Mead's interest in the ferments from papaya and their medical potential led to his de-

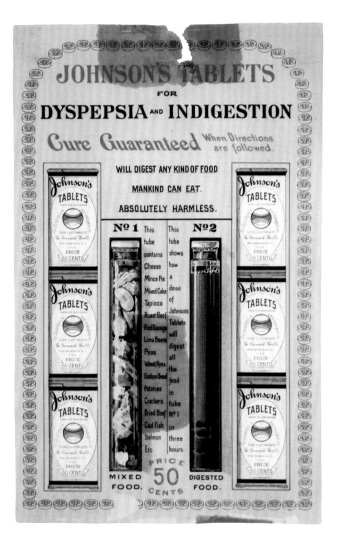

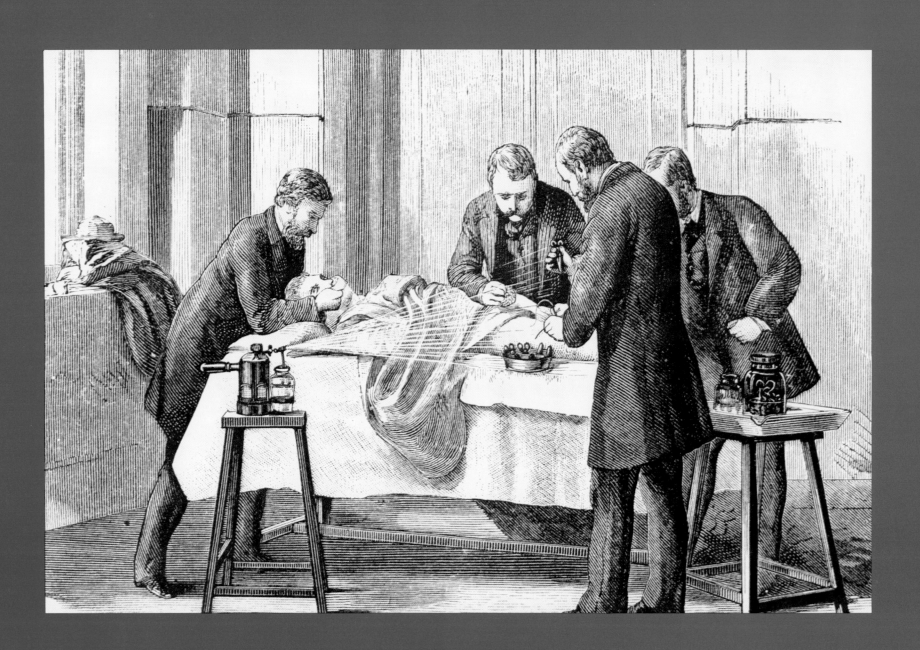

Once the mystery of patient infection was solved, attention was focused on all of its possible causes. None was of greater concern than the suture material used to close wounds and incisions. Selecting the right material for sutures was critical, for it had to be strong and readily absorbed by the body.

In 1865 Lister tried using ordinary musical instrument strings made from sheep intestines. They worked, though ironically Lister had to settle for inferior quality because all of the best strings were saved for use in musical instruments. The material was known as "catgut," and making it sterile was exceedingly difficult. The more that catgut was treated the greater danger there was that its natural properties would be destroyed. Catgut sutures were among JOHNSON & JOHNSON's earliest products. With them began

an endless effort to improve suture quality and the methods used to sterilize it.

The goal was to achieve fineness, tensile strength and pliability without resorting to the use of chemicals that would alter the organic state of the material. The complicated process developed by the Company for sterilizing sutures called for immersing the catgut in a corrosive solution, then letting it set for ten days in oil of juniper berries. The strings were then packaged in vials with a twenty percent alcohol solution. At the time, many physicians were purchasing sutures and ligatures directly from drug stores since much of the surgery they performed was done in their offices or the homes of patients.

The new suturing material brought a grateful response from physicians. "As to sutures," one surgeon wrote, "I have used common sewing thread many times in lieu of anything better, and oh dear how I as well as the patient counted the days when they must be removed." Within a short time physicians would have a choice of nine types of catgut and twenty-one silk sutures from JOHNSON & JOHNSON.

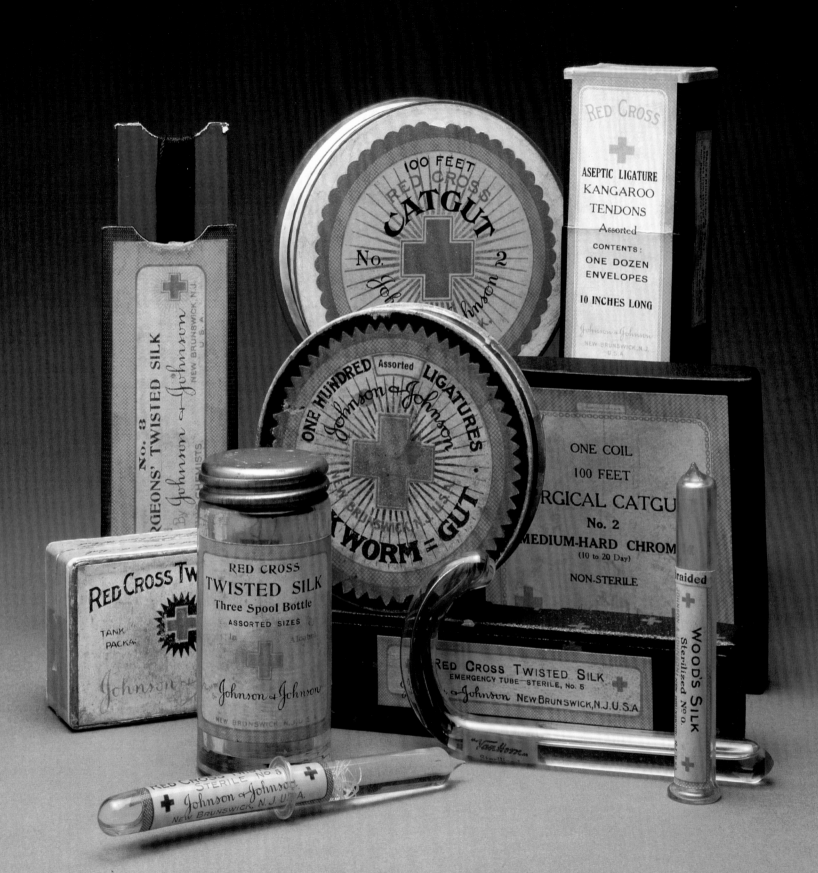

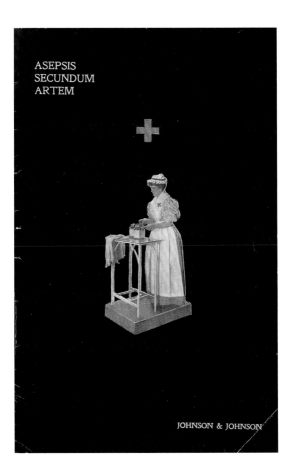

JOHNSON & JOHNSON

The early research laboratories had grown in size as well as expertise, and in 1896 the Company proudly proclaimed:

"The scientific department of JOHNSON & JOHNSON as amplified, strengthened and extended, is probably unique in the purpose of the work accomplished. Employed is a staff of skilled workers in chemistry, bacteriology, pharmacology, and allied sciences. They are equipped with all the appliances and apparatus that modern science affords. Eminent specialists in surgery, medicine and hygiene have augmented the work of the laboratory by clinical experiments and by practical application. Through this source new preparations and improvements on old ones have been tested before recommendation to the medical profession. Workers keep in touch with every stage of progress in the science of medicine, surgery and sanitation. This is carried out whether the subject may be closely or remotely connected with the industry."

Kilmer continued making scholarly contributions to medical literature. The most important paper of his career was issued in 1897 and titled *Asepsis Secundum Artem.* Hailed as the outstanding monograph of the year, it was considered a classic on the subject of sterility in wound care and the single most important paper ever written on asepsis. Much of the scientific data in the paper had been developed in the Bacteriological Laboratory that JOHNSON & JOHNSON had built to test various germicidal processes and other preventive measures calculated to enhance sterility. This new knowledge led to the development of the largest sterilizer ever built, capable of holding six truckloads of surgical dressings at one time.

Maternity and obstetric kits became an important part of the JOHNSON & JOHNSON product line, and remained so for years. They played a vital role in the safe birth of tens of thousands of babies, the majority of whom were born at home. If the mothers-to-be were fortunate enough to have the assistance of a physician at birth, the risks were greatly reduced. Often these duties were performed by a midwife, some of whom had special training. It was a fortunate mother who had both a physician and midwife assisting at the birth.

The contents of the maternity and obstetric kits improved greatly over the years, and the Company relied heavily on the advice of physicians, often naming the kit for a doctor who had aided most in its development. Dr. Simpson's Maternity Packet, sold by druggists for $3.00, included an obstetric sheet, cotton and gauze, silk ligatures for tying the umbilical cord (with a square knot), antiseptic soap and muslin binders for both mother and infant. A maternity kit suggested by Dr. Joseph Brown Cooke, surgeon at the New York Maternity Hospital, was more elaborate and more expensive and contained sanitary napkins for the mother, a relatively new product at the time.

The Johnson's First Dressing Packet for Infants sold for $4.00 and included an extensive array of products. Perhaps most important was nitrate of silver solution and instructions for using it in babies' eyes to prevent the dreaded infections that so often led to blindness. Detailed instructions went with all of the kits, and most of the cautions were aimed directly at preventing various types of infection in the child or mother during the critical days after birth. A slogan, "Every child has the right to be born well," was used in the literature repeatedly, and served as a constant reminder of the perils of birth before the advent of modern medicine.

Robert, Evangeline, and Seward

When Robert Johnson was forty-seven he married for the second time. His first marriage was brief and had ended in divorce. His new bride was Evangeline Armstrong, some twenty years younger and disarmingly attractive. They were married in a quiet ceremony at Maryville, Tennessee, on June 27, 1892. After the honeymoon they returned to New Brunswick and moved into a spacious house that Johnson had bought for $75,000.

Gray Terrace, as the house was called, was an opulent and rather awkward looking mansion in the Victorian style. It loomed somewhat pretentiously behind a stone wall topped by decorative wrought iron. The house, horse barns and greenhouses were on several acres at the corner of College Avenue and Hamilton Street, just across from the Rutgers University campus and a block away from Johnson's factories. Within a span of five years the couple had three children, Robert Wood Johnson, the second, born April 4, 1893; John Seward, born July 14, 1895; and Evangeline Brewster, born April 18, 1897. Roberta, Johnson's daughter by his previous marriage, also lived with them.

Despite its somewhat forbidding appearance, Gray Terrace was a happy home, with the four Johnson children frolicking through its cavernous rooms and watched over by a household staff of five. On the grounds at the rear of the house there were greenhouses filled with the orchids that Johnson raised, and horse barns, where "Dandy," the children's pony, was kept. The pony would be hitched to a handsome black cart and the children would take endless turns around the grounds, urging "Dandy" on to greater speed.

In the early 1890s Johnson was drawing a monthly salary of only $800. Instead of draining the Company's cash reserves he preferred to add to his JOHNSON & JOHNSON stock holdings. Once he transferred two patents he held for product improvements in exchange for 50,000 shares. He was also a shrewd investor in the stock market, often making several transactions a week that added significantly to his growing wealth.

The sinking of the U.S. battleship *Maine* in Havana Harbor in 1898 led to the Spanish-American War and the Company's first involvement in supplying the military. To the beat of John Philip Sousa's "Stars and Stripes Forever," some 150,000 volunteers signed up to help free Cuba and other possessions from Spanish rule.

On the day that war was declared Robert Johnson wrote to Richard Gwathmey, a Company salesman from Virginia, who was the first employee to volunteer for military service. "We not only most heartily applaud your action," Johnson said, "but we will be glad to render you every assistance in our power. Not only will we be glad to keep your place open for you, but will also continue your pay, the same as heretofore, during your entire absence." Gwathmey was elated, and when he arrived at Camp Cuba Libra in Virginia he promptly wrote to all of his customers praising the Company's generosity and asking for their continued orders.

The threat of war touched off a frenzy of activity at the factory. Over 300,000 packets of a newly developed compressed surgical dressing for use in the field were produced for the Army and Navy. When 18,000 American troops went ashore in Cuba they carried a new type of cloth stretcher designed and produced by JOHNSON & JOHNSON. Workers subscribed $100,000 to the War Loan drive, and when the ambulance ship *U.S. Solace* sailed for Cuba it carried a huge quantity of medical supplies donated by the Company.

Speaking for the Company, Kilmer pledged: "Millions of pounds of cotton, millions of yards of gauze, miles upon miles of bandages, plasters enough to encircle the earth…they are yours, Uncle Sam, if you need them, and they are made 'Secundum Artem Asepsis'" (Following the Art of Asepsis).

Fortunately, the conflict ended quickly. When soldiers and sailors arrived home they were greeted by a popular new song, "When Johnny Comes Marching Home."

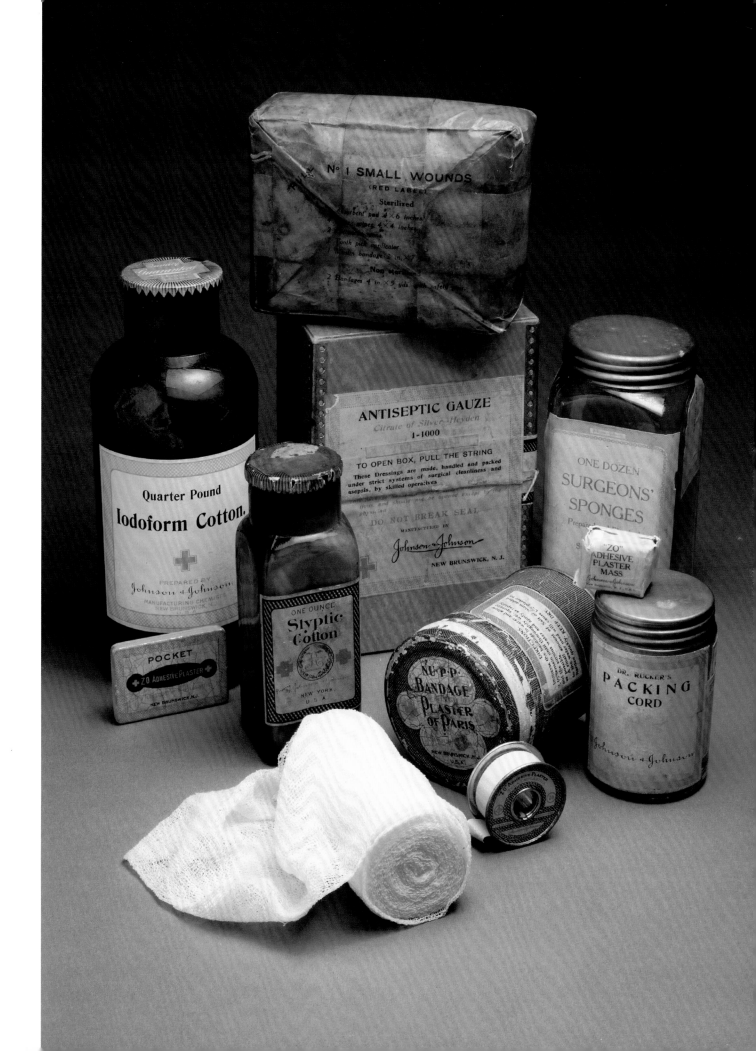

In the late afternoon of September 5, 1901, while greeting people at the Pan American Exposition in Buffalo, New York, President William McKinley was shot twice by a young anarchist who had concealed a gun in his bandaged right hand. Aides rushed McKinley by ambulance to the Exposition's well-equipped infirmary. He was in shock, but conscious. As McKinley was being examined, one bullet fell out of his clothing, apparently deflected by a button. The other had cut a path through his stomach and was lost in the muscles of his back. Attending physicians decided to operate immediately in a vain attempt to save the President's life, but he died a week later. Ironically, newly developed X-ray equipment was on exhibit elsewhere at the Exposition. Had it been used on McKinley, surgeons might have been able to locate and remove the bullet that took his life.

McKinley's medical case became the topic of nationwide discussion. Could the life of the popular President have been saved? In the next issue of *Red Cross Notes*, the publication for physicians, JOHNSON & JOHNSON presented a detailed clinical explanation of the McKinley case, complete with anatomical diagrams. It was an attempt to use the famous case to instruct physicians how to deal with bullet wounds of this gravity. The autopsy had already exonerated the medical team, but it was felt that a wider knowledge of the case would aid in the future treatment of abdominal wounds of this type. In the article Kilmer presented extensive excerpts from the official records, then added philosophically: "…though nations come and go,

republics flourish or wither, rulers pass away, the healing art moves on, and the surgeons will turn from the keen disappointment as to the outcome of this illustrious case to a study of the scientific aspects." It had been determined that throughout McKinley's ordeal JOHNSON & JOHNSON products—sterile dressings and sutures—had been used in the operation.

A year earlier JOHNSON & JOHNSON products had played an important role in another tragedy. On September 8, 1900, a devastating storm struck Galveston, Texas, destroying nearly one-third of the city and wreaking havoc for miles around. The storm-tossed Gulf of Mexico, propelled by winds exceeding 100 miles per hour, came crashing into the city in fifteen-foot waves, demolishing homes and businesses and leaving a death toll of 6,000. Emergency medical teams, including the indomitable eighty-year-old Clara Barton, were severely hampered by a shortage of medical supplies. At first news of the disaster the Company sent emergency medical supplies and offered aid to physicians, druggists and their families.

It was Robert Johnson's nature to worry about the competition. He once learned that Bauer & Black, a new firm formed by one of his former sales managers, S. H. Black, was doing very well. Johnson was skeptical, so he wrote to his Chicago sales representative:

"I wish you would learn if Bauer & Black are as busy as they claim to be, even if you have to hire someone to watch their factory at night."

A lesser annoyance was the tiny Lister Company, whose principal reputation was as a notorious price cutter. Johnson bought it out for $2,000. A far more serious threat, however, was posed by the J. Ellwood Lee Company of Conshohocken, Pennsylvania. That firm produced a complete line of sutures and ligatures, medicinal plasters, catheters, trusses and numerous other products similar to those in Johnson's line. J. Ellwood Lee, a born entrepreneur, was no pushover, and Johnson knew it. Lee's company had become a major

factor in the drug trade, and for some time had been cutting prices sharply. Johnson wrote to Lee: "If you follow the start you have made, in a short time you will be giving away goods and paying people to take them. When you get tired of this fun, come down to Cape May, take a bath and cool off."

In 1905 Johnson acquired the Lee company in exchange for JOHNSON & JOHNSON stock. It was the first major acquisition, and under terms of the arrangement both companies would list the other's products in their catalogs and continue their independent ways. Lee and two of his associates, Charles Heber Clark and Frank R. Jones, joined the JOHNSON & JOHNSON Board. Clark, writing under the pen name of Max Adeler, was one of the leading humorists of the day. When Lee was very young Clark had helped him obtain his first job by writing and placing a newspaper ad for him in a Philadelphia newspaper. In gratitude, years later, Lee made Clark a member of his board when he formed his own company. About Lee, Clark wrote: "The founder of our business is in many particulars an unusual man. He has inventive power, which when applied to the needs of his business, has produced important consequences not only for himself, but for surgical science."

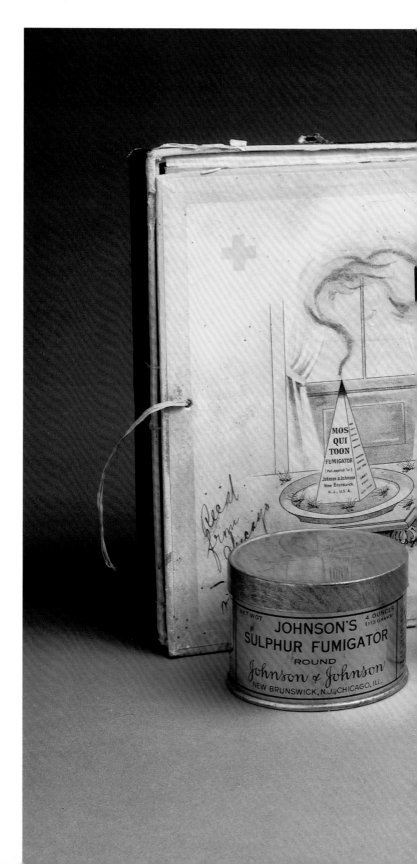

Following the merger of the two firms, Kilmer prepared a booklet called *Handbook of Ligatures,* and Clark collaborated in writing it. It soon gained wide acceptance in hospitals and among surgeons. In it the authors proudly proclaimed: "These firms control the entire process," and indeed they did.

Five years after joining Johnson, Lee turned his attention to a new pursuit, the construction of a block long, four-story factory in Pennsylvania for the production of tires for the infant auto industry. That also put Johnson in the tire business but he soon became disenchanted with it; Henry Ford helped. Lee marketed a brand of tire he called Jelco, a name derived from his initials. Ford expressed dismay at having his autos riding around on tires bearing a name that suggested "jelly" to owners and prospective owners, so Lee promptly changed the name of the tire to "Lee of Conshohocken." Eventually, all connections between Johnson's company and the Lee Tire and Rubber Company were severed, though it continued marketing tires for many years.

Very little attention had been paid to developing first aid products and techniques until JOHNSON & JOHNSON began its pioneering efforts in the late 1800s. The inspiration for Robert Johnson's decision to enter the first aid business came from an unlikely source: the nation's rapidly expanding network of railroads.

Johnson was part owner of a cattle ranch in Colorado, where he spent his vacations. On trips there by rail he often spoke with the chief surgeon of the Denver and Rio Grande Railway about the frequency and severity of railroad accidents. At that time there was a frantic effort to complete the 100,000 miles of railroad track criss-crossing the country. Much of the trackage had to be laid through hazardous terrain, and the accident rate among rail workers was appallingly high. The more he

learned about railroad injuries and accidents the more interested Johnson became in the need to have a supply of medical products on hand. After getting advice from other railway surgeons, Johnson developed the nation's first Railway Station and Factory Supply Case in 1890. It was a large wooden case containing an ample assortment of antiseptic dressings, surgical supplies, splints and other medical aids. The Company recommended that the railroad kit be placed with station agents so that it could be available to send to the scene of an accident.

The instructions that came with the kit included some grim advice on providing first aid for severed fingers, toes and legs, and, quite appropriately, told how to treat people who had fainted. "If the accident is serious," the instructions warned, "send for a surgeon at once. While waiting, keep cool."

Hanging like a dark cloud over early attempts at applying first aid was the ever present danger that the well meaning volunteer would further injure the victim by applying the wrong

technique. Others argued that even rudimentary first aid was better than none at all. Realizing that effective first aid required knowledge as much as products, JOHNSON & JOHNSON began the most intensive study of the subject ever undertaken. When it was completed a decade or more later, the Company would be able to set the standards for all future first aid techniques.

It remained for Fred Kilmer to come up with an accepted definition of first aid, which also carried with it a caution. "First aid," he said, "is meant to prevent an extension of an injury rather than its treatment."

From the railroad kit, the Company went on to produce a long line of first aid kits for use on the farm, in the home, school, office and factory. Later there was one for the auto, and even the airplane. Having a JOHNSON & JOHNSON First Aid Kit on hand for emergencies soon became a necessity for many.

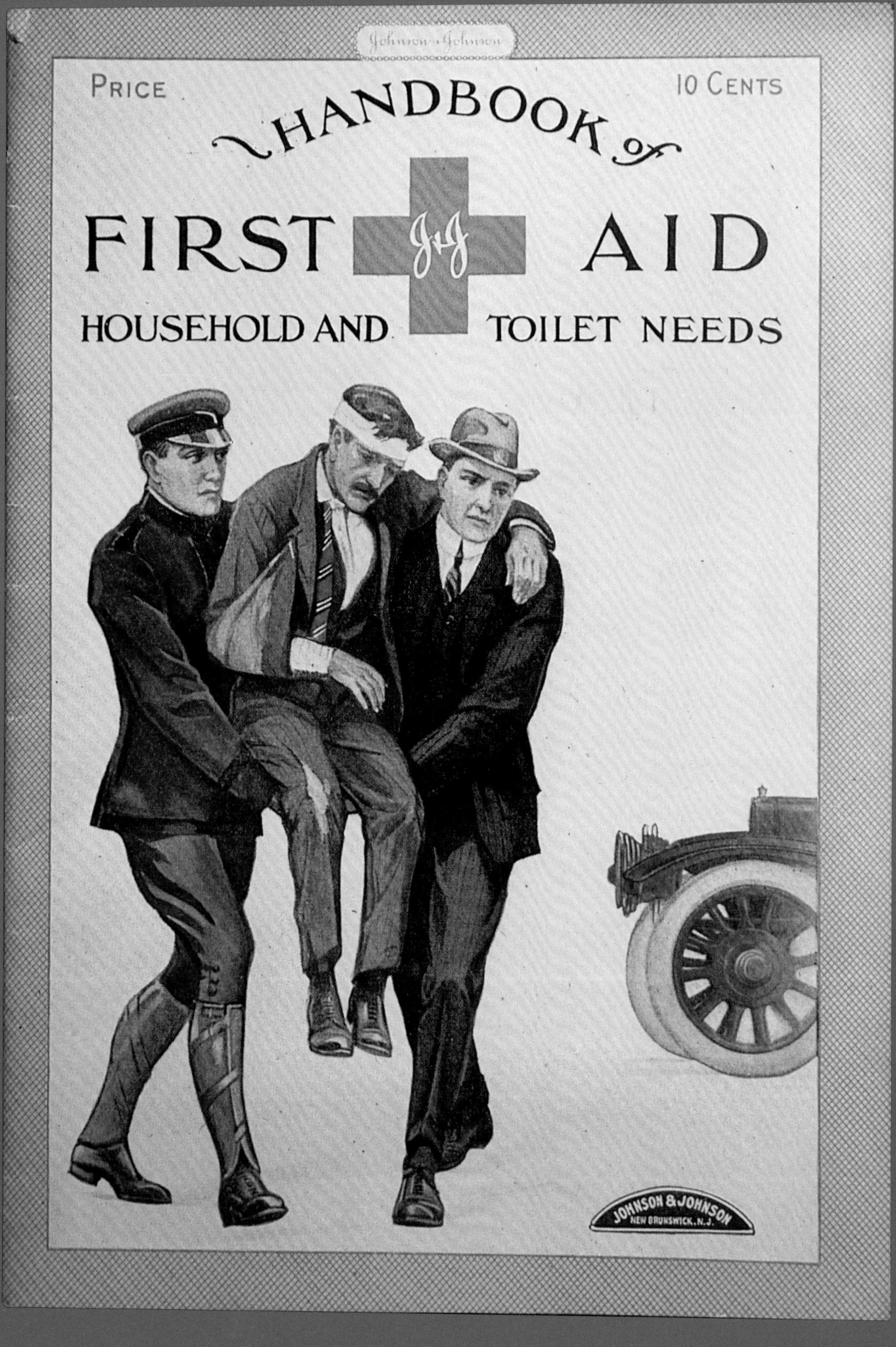
Johnson & Johnson
PRICE
10 CENTS
HANDBOOK of
FIRST
J&J
AID
HOUSEHOLD AND
TOILET NEEDS
JOHNSON & JOHNSON
NEW BRUNSWICK, N.J.

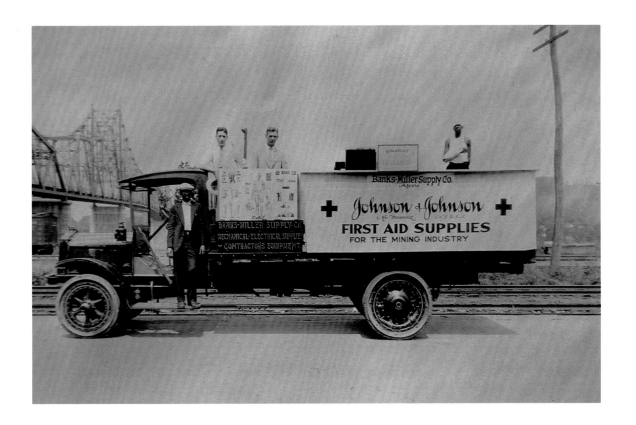

As industry expanded and production machinery became more complex, accident rates climbed rapidly. The same held true on the newly mechanized farms, and in transportation systems that moved people at even higher speeds. More accidents naturally increased the need for better first aid techniques and trained people to learn them. Volunteer teams were recruited and trained in factories and communities all over the nation.

As JOHNSON & JOHNSON learned more about first aid a series of detailed bulletins was prepared on how to treat specific injuries. In one of the bulletins Kilmer expanded on his earlier definition of first aid, calling it "a bridge between the accident and medical and surgical assistance, over which the patient may be carried safely and securely from the scene of the accident or sudden illness to the doctor or hospital…"

In 1901 the Company published the first complete book ever written on the subject, *Johnson's First Aid Manual.* It dealt with the simplest, most effective methods for laymen to treat the injured in an emergency, while keeping in mind the caution that the ultimate fate of the injured person often depended on the actions of the first person to apply first aid. The right technique could be most helpful, while the wrong action could be fatal. Each recommended step was carefully illustrated to avoid errors, and as Kilmer noted in his introduction, "Extensiveness has in all cases been sacrificed to simplicity."

The manual, which sold for fifty cents, was an immediate success. Soon it was adopted by thousands of first aid training programs as the "official" guide. Equally important, the book helped to focus attention on the improvement of first aid techniques. As a result, when the eighth edition of the guide went to press a decade later, there were contributions from sixty-five physicians, each of them dealing with a different and often new aspect of first aid. A leading medical journal, *American Medicine,* hailed the manual as the most complete book of its kind, and gave an added compliment to JOHNSON & JOHNSON for never having attempted "to give instruction in surgery."

When the San Francisco earthquake struck on April 18, 1906, JOHNSON & JOHNSON products were rushed to treat victims of a disaster in which the Company itself was a victim. At 5:20 that morning an earthquake registering 8.3 on the Richter Scale leveled large portions of downtown San Francisco. The quake touched off dozens of fires that raged out of control. By ten o'clock fire had destroyed what remained of the warehouse and offices of Waldron & Dietrich at 144 Second Street, the JOHNSON & JOHNSON agents for the

Pacific Coast. Immediately the Waldron people got permission from the Red Cross to telegraph an urgent appeal to JOHNSON & JOHNSON in New Brunswick for emergency medical supplies.

By the end of the day, rail cars were filled with products at New Brunswick and other Company warehouse locations. Within hours they were on their way to the stricken city. The holocaust continued for three days, and many buildings had to be dynamited to keep the inferno from spreading. Thousands were injured and the death toll climbed to 452. Soon the first of the medical supplies donated by JOHNSON & JOHNSON arrived to treat the survivors. Later, the

Company was informed that it had donated the largest amount of medical supplies sent to San Francisco. This was to become common practice in later years when disasters struck.

To assist druggists trying to recover from earthquake damage, the Company cancelled all invoices under $100. And following the devastating flood in Galveston, Texas, several years earlier, all damaged JOHNSON & JOHNSON products in drugstores had been replaced by the Company at no cost. Actions like these firmly established the Company's growing reputation among its trade customers. These practices generated enormous good will, as one grateful druggist wrote: "…permit me to offer you my service whenever you need it, and any command will be gladly obeyed." The good will was also reflected in the Company's growing success. That year's sales were nearly $3 million, rising from just $1 million seven years earlier.

New ideas quickly blossomed into new products. Johnson continued to concentrate on marketing strategies, strengthening the sales organization, new packaging, and product quality. On that score Kilmer observed: "He was firm in the belief that high quality and handsome packages were valuable factors in obtaining trade support and holding the good will of his patrons."

Johnson's emphasis on quality, combined with his constant demands for perfection, made him the taskmaster of the organization. Things had to be done to his complete satisfaction, and where product quality was concerned he would not permit compromise. He was difficult to please, but no one disputed the results he achieved in sales and profits. He watched sales figures daily, guarding them carefully, and when he thought too much information was getting to competitors he took action. "Sales for March will be from ten to fifteen percent higher than the same month last year," he wrote a traveler. "This I do not care to mention outside, but prefer to state that we are barely holding our own in sales."

By now the drugstores of America had become a national institution. Their familiar red and green show globes in the display windows served as beacons for all in search of medications. The tens of thousands of drugstores across the country were remarkably similar, with perfume and cigar counters, huge glass and wood display cases, and walls of gleaming mahogany with dozens of small drawers that held secrets only the proprietor knew about. At the rear of the store the pharmacist communed with his mortar and pestle and his compounds in isolation behind a discreet glass partition. Then came the invasion of the soda fountain, with its marble and onyx top, its swirly wirebacked chairs and whirring ice cream mixer. Many diehard druggists resisted creating a social center for young romantics, but the more enterprising grasped the opportunity to lure new customers into their store.

A close rapport had been established between the Company and druggists of the nation, for in addition to serving vast numbers of consumers the drugstore was also a prime source of supply for physicians and dentists. JOHNSON & JOHNSON's dental business grew rapidly after 1898 when Dr. Burt Simmons, a genial and imaginative dentist, joined the Company. Not long after his arrival he invented Cottonoid, tightly packed rolls of cotton that dentists stuffed in patients' mouths to keep dry the area where they were working. Like Kilmer, Dr. Simmons was zealous in pursuit of his professional goals, one of which was better oral hygiene. He organized a series of community health events on behalf of dentists which he called "Aseptic Day," and though his slogans were ominous — "Men and women are doomed to constantly combat dirt, disease and the devil" — they were effective.

About this time the Company introduced a new publication for druggists, which it called *Red Cross Messenger*. Its stated goal was to help the drugstore "sell more goods and make better profits," an objective that got little argument. The *Messenger* was an immediate success, with a circulation of some 50,000 copies. There was something in the monthly issues for everyone behind the drugstore counter: blandishments for the seasoned pharmacist: "He is an educator and ranks with the clergyman, the teacher and the physician," and encouragement for his young apprentices: "Grover Cleveland was a druggist." Through the publication, a Clerk's Club was formed using the motto "Keep To The Front."

The *Messenger* began devoting columns to the Women's Organization of the National Association of Retail Druggists, a group formed to promote a closer association among druggists' families, and also a strong proponent of suffragette causes. Under the heading "Leaders in The Woman's Movement," the *Messenger* carried letters and articles objecting to advertising that took advantage of women. As a result, the publication became increasingly popular. When Company salesmen called on druggists, articles that had appeared in the *Messenger* were a topic of discussion and an easy bridge to the more serious business of selling JOHNSON & JOHNSON products.

JOHNSON & JOHNSON'S
ASEPTIC DENTAL SPECIALTIES

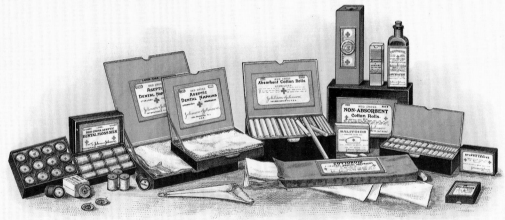

STERILIZED AND SURGICALLY CLEAN

Cotton Rolls **Aseptic Napkins** **Cottonoid**

FOR SALE HERE

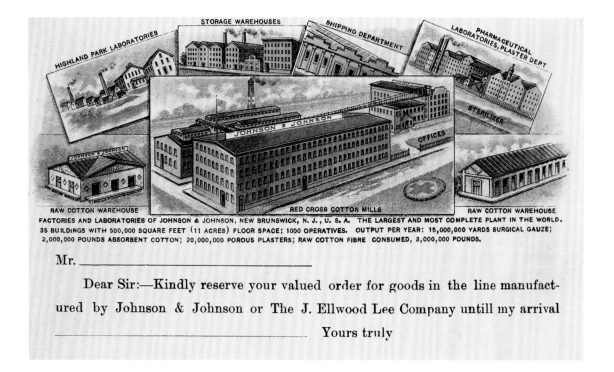

HIGHLAND PARK LABORATORIES

STORAGE WAREHOUSES

SHIPPING DEPARTMENT

PHARMACEUTICAL LABORATORIES, PLASTER DEPT

JOHNSON & JOHNSON

STERILIZER

OFFICES

JOHNSON & JOHNSON

RAW COTTON WAREHOUSE

RED CROSS COTTON MILLS

RAW COTTON WAREHOUSE

FACTORIES AND LABORATORIES OF JOHNSON & JOHNSON, NEW BRUNSWICK, N. J., U. S. A. THE LARGEST AND MOST COMPLETE PLANT IN THE WORLD. 35 BUILDINGS WITH 500,000 SQUARE FEET (11 ACRES) FLOOR SPACE; 1000 OPERATIVES. OUTPUT PER YEAR: 15,000,000 YARDS SURGICAL GAUZE; 2,000,000 POUNDS ABSORBENT COTTON; 20,000,000 POROUS PLASTERS; RAW COTTON FIBRE CONSUMED, 3,000,000 POUNDS.

Mr. _____

Dear Sir:—Kindly reserve your valued order for goods in the line manufactured by Johnson & Johnson or The J. Ellwood Lee Company untill my arrival _____ Yours truly

The Company played an important role in the drafting of the National Pure Food & Drugs Act in 1906, described as "the country's first attempt at curbing the mounting abuses in the mass production of foods, drugs, medicines and liquors." Kilmer described it as a "righteous law," adding that it was "the most important and far reaching example of

Federal legislation placed upon our statute books since the period of the Civil War."

Before the law was enacted, the public had not been protected in its eagerness to buy the new processed foods and medicinal products that came streaming into the market. Higher factory production brought increasing abuses, as the nation moved farther away from having the home serve as the principal supplier of food, clothing, and homemade medicinal remedies. For every mass producer of goods that adhered to careful quality and production controls

there was an unscrupulous manufacturer ready to cut corners and, even worse, endanger health.

While stories of sickness and death from contaminated food and drugs abounded throughout the nation, they had not come into sharp enough focus to ignite action by authorities. It remained for author Upton Sinclair to light that fuse in 1906, with publication of his muckraker novel, *The Jungle.* The book graphically described the exploitation of immigrant labor employed in the stockyards and the nauseating methods of killing animals and preparing the meat for consumption.

Sinclair was an enthusiastic supporter of socialism and other causes, and intended that his novel would generate sympathy for the workers, which it did. But it also generated a greater national concern for the plight of the consumer. Another author, Samuel Hopkins Adams, directed attention to the need for food and drug controls in his book, *The Great American Fraud,* and in a series of articles he wrote for *Collier's* magazine exposing quack patent medicines.

When a commission appointed to investigate the methods of food preparation verified the most shocking revelations in the two books, President Theodore Roosevelt and Congress were prodded into action. Roosevelt appointed Harvey W. Wiley, a strong proponent of the reforms, to administer the Pure Food and Drugs Act once it was put in workable form. This called for an evaluation of the right controls, and Kilmer's expert advice was promptly sought since he was a recognized authority in the field of public health.

The magnitude of the national problem that the act attempted to correct was evident in its title: "An act for preventing the manufacture, sale or transportation of adulterated or misbranded or poisonous or deleterious foods, drugs, medicines, and liquors, and for regulating traffic therein, and for other purposes." It was passed by Congress on June 30, 1906. While the Pure Food and Drugs Act provided only weak penalties for violators, its impact on the nation was profound. It succeeded in screening from the marketplace countless foods and drug preparations that first had to pass tests in special

Fred B. Kilmer

government laboratories set up for the purpose. Many inferior products that slipped through were later removed from the market by a band of food inspectors who fanned out across the nation. This touched off widespread concern over whether certain substances used in food and drugs were harmful to public health. The debate raged on for years.

JOHNSON & JOHNSON was assigned "No. 117—Guaranteed Under the Food and Drugs Act," which, signed by Johnson himself, gave assurance that these products were not adulterated or misbranded.

Passage of the new Pure Food & Drug Act was described by Fred Kilmer as "a marvelous revolution in the statements made by the proprietors of 'patent' or proprietary remedies and 'quack' medicines." The new law came as a jolt to some firms, and many questionable products soon disappeared from the market.

When tested, every product produced by JOHNSON & JOHNSON turned out to be in full conformity with the law and no changes in production methods or standards were required. At the request of the government, the Company made available to the Department of Agriculture, which had responsibility for the analysis of products, all of the testing procedures and techniques that had been developed in the laboratories over the years.

Kilmer had always seen his and the Company's mission in health care as extending beyond products. He described that larger role quite eloquently: "The department is not conducted in any narrow, commercial spirit, but is constantly engaged in purely scientific inquiry, and not kept going for the purpose of paying dividends or solely for the benefit of JOHNSON & JOHNSON, but a view to aiding the progress of the art of healing."

Beyond the immediate impact that the new Act had on public health was its influence in bringing about improvements in state and local laws. Almost immediately there was increased pressure on government authorities to do something about serious health conditions, including the chlorination of water, inspection of milk, control of flies and mosquitos, and regulations to decrease the spread of diphtheria and tuberculosis. Many of these measures, including the relatively new practice of giving physical examinations to school children, were part of the program already initiated by Fred Kilmer in his service as a public health official in New Jersey at the state and local levels. What remained to be done was to educate authorities on the

wisdom of tightening health laws, and Kilmer and his associates went about the task vigorously. He later recalled their efforts to bring about health reforms: "Our work was largely educational, but out of these crude and faulty methods came the great advances in hygiene and sanitation, including improvement in the water supply, increased sewage disposal, tuberculosis campaigns, care of babies, visiting nurse programs, and a whole host of measures calculated to improve the health of our citizens."

In 1907 the nation was beset by a devastating depression that brought unemployment and hardship to many. JOHNSON & JOHNSON managed to weather the storm, and even continue the program of plant expansion. There were belt-tightening measures in the form of shorter hours and lower paychecks, but few jobs were lost. The causes of the panic reflected some serious flaws in the American economic structure, including an inefficient credit system and too much "water" in the capital structures of the railroads and the new trusts. High profits, contrasting

THE HOME NEWS

SATURDAY, OCTOBER 3, 1908.

2,500 PEOPLE INAUGURATE J. & J.'S NEW MILL

Monster Housewarming Marks the Completion of Newest Addition to the Great Works —Officers and Wives Present—Congratulations From President Johnson.

Nearly twent

with the low wages of workers, resulted in low buying power and this led to considerable speculation about mismanagement during the boom years from 1898 to 1907.

On the night of October 2, 1908, over 2,500 of Johnson's workers gathered to celebrate the dedication of the new addition to the Red Cross Cotton Mill, which now brought the complex to forty buildings and a half million square feet of manufacturing space. It was a festive evening, and the music and laughter contrasted sharply with the sad economic refrain of the previous year.

"Above all, we hope that the future will bring back the prosperity that has been missing for the past year," Johnson told his employees. "You have put forth your best effort loyally and jointly… observing all the rules relating to modern wound dressings. When the products reach the surgeon he has absolute confidence in them. We have been educators, teaching the world how to treat wounds according to modern methods and how to save life."

"This factory is now undoubtedly the largest in the world…," he said, "…and in the very near future we may be able to provide still further for the welfare and comfort of every employee."

A newspaper report of the celebration said: "brain workers mixed easily with those who toil with their hands, and all were aglow with good humor and fraught with a feeling of fraternity."

DAILY HOME NEWS

New Brunswick, N. J.

MONDAY, FEBRUARY 7, 1910.

DEATH CALLS A CAPTAIN OF INDUSTRY

Robert W. Johnson, President of the World Famous Johnson & Johnson Company, Succumbs at the Age of 65—Left Business Last Monday Ill—Bright's Disease Brought the End.

Robert Wood Johnson died at 6.40 this morning at his residence, College avenue and Hamilton street, surrounded by all his family and near relatives. He had been unconscious for some time be-

Robert Johnson's sudden illness and death came as a tremendous shock, for he had always been in robust health. He dealt with minor illnesses with the same dispatch with which he handled other annoying problems, but there were times when the rapidly expanding business weighed heavily on him. "I have so many strings on my bow that I can hardly manage the bow at all," he commented shortly before his illness.

The first hint of Johnson's sickness came on the morning of January 31, 1910, when he left the office early complaining of not feeling well. That was rare for him. The following day was the Company's annual stockholder meeting, and Johnson was not well enough to attend. Two days later he was diagnosed as having an acute kidney ailment.

A growing despair pressed down on Gray Terrace. Those who passed in and out of the big house moved quickly on their anxious missions, as though their own bursts of energy could somehow be transmitted to the rapidly declining Johnson. On the sixth day of his illness he slipped into unconsciousness. At daybreak on February 7th doctors summoned the family to Johnson's bedside, and he died soon afterward.

Among Johnson's 2,500 workers there was a pervading sense of doom and foreboding, for many were convinced that the Company could not continue to be successful without his leadership. On Wednesday morning 1,200 of Johnson's employees gathered at the factory and began moving slowly up Hamilton Street in double file to Gray Terrace. All morning long they moved through the gates of the big house and through the drawing room where the body reposed in a gleaming mahogany casket exactly the same as the one in which President McKinley had been buried.

There were hundreds of floral pieces, from a modest bouquet from the orphans of St. Mary's Home to a massive arrangement of 2,000 pink roses from the family. It was the largest funeral in the city's history.

Ten days later the Board of Directors selected Johnson's brother, James, to succeed him as President. Responding to the call, "Uncle Jimmy," as he was affectionately known around the Company, wrote to each of his employees as follows:

…"I take this occasion to assure you that there will be no change either in the policy and conduct of the business or in the energy and vigor with which it will be prosecuted…My policy was my brother's policy. My brother's policy is my policy."

James W. Johnson

In the weeks following Johnson's death speculation was rampant over the size of his estate and how it would be divided. When the will was probated the value was placed at more than $2 million. Johnson made generous provisions for his widow and children, but left his vast common stock holdings in JOHNSON & JOHNSON in trust for his two sons. Soon after his death his widow, Evangeline, moved to New York City and enrolled the two youngest children, Seward and Evangeline, in private schools there. Robert, then sixteen, remained in New Brunswick and continued his education at Rutgers Preparatory School.

The boy and his father had been very close. When other children his age were playing carefree games, Robert would accompany his father to business meetings and sit and listen. When he was in his early teens Robert decided that someday he would enter the family business and follow in his father's footsteps; his father's sudden death required him to make that decision much earlier than anticipated.

That June, Robert took a summer job at the factory and became friendly with many of the workers. In the fall he returned to Rutgers Prep for his senior year. When he graduated the following spring he announced that he was not going to college, but instead would be taking a full-time job at JOHNSON & JOHNSON. His mother and uncle registered strong objections, then finally relented and allowed Robert to begin working. His first job was in the factory power plant, but then he began moving from one department to another, staying just long enough to learn each one's functions. Along the way he continued his easy rapport with the workers, particularly the Hungarian immigrants, who soon adopted him as one of their own.

New Brunswick had become a center of Hungarian life in the United States. Hungarians had begun arriving in large numbers about 1850, after their defeat by the Austrian Hapsburg forces, aided by the intervention of Czarist Russia. At one time more than a third of New Brunswick's population could trace their origins to Hungary, and the city became known as "the most Hungarian City in the United States." The Hungarians were hardworking, honest, and fiercely loyal, and in time comprised more than two-thirds of the JOHNSON & JOHNSON work force, to the point where the Company became known as "Hungarian University."

Robert W. Johnson

J&J Hiker's Club.

68 – L

As President, James Johnson kept his word about following the policies of his brother. Though less flamboyant than Robert, he nonetheless asserted a quiet leadership that commanded the respect of his employees and made the transition far less traumatic than had been expected. One of his first actions was to expand the services of the Company Welfare Department that had been formed in 1906. The department was widely hailed as a revolutionary step forward in employee benefits, and came at a time when many workers all across the nation were loudly protesting poor working conditions that endangered both safety and health. By contrast, the program at JOHNSON & JOHNSON was a huge advance in employee relations.

Hospital and retiring rooms were set up to care for those taken ill on the job. Physicians and nurses gave treatment and advice on medical problems, often referring employees to local doctors and arranging for the bill to be paid by the Company. A legal and counseling service dealt with marital and family problems. A mutual benefit fund was established to provide financial support during illness and other family crises.

Classes were organized in hygiene, gymnastics, millinery, embroidery and instruction in English. In 1907 women employees formed the Laurel Club for their social and educational enjoyment. They had a basketball team, a Glee Club and a lending library, and the monthly dues of twenty-five cents helped support the club's charity work at St. Peter's Orphanage.

The Company bought three blocks of houses in New Brunswick, reconditioned them and rented thirty-two fully equipped homes to factory workers at reasonable rents. Maintenance costs were borne by the Company.

To make working the night shift more appealing the Company hired a French chef to prepare appetizing hot meals which were served at midnight with great flourish. Later JOHNSON & JOHNSON became one of the first companies to provide pensions and insurance coverage for many of its employees.

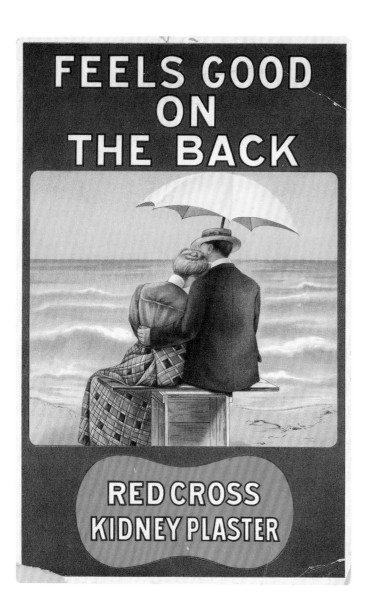

FEELS GOOD
ON
THE BACK

RED CROSS
KIDNEY PLASTER

Advertising was becoming a new force in American business in the years just before World War I. During the war, advertising would reach new pinnacles of success in arousing patriotic spirit in the nation to a crescendo. But in the pre-war years, before the advent of high-speed, four-color magazine presses and radio commercials, there were few memorable advertising campaigns. And the reasons why some were so highly successful often remained a mystery. One of the most successful, and the most baffling, was launched by JOHNSON & JOHNSON on behalf of one of its oldest products, kidney plasters.

There was no more unlikely candidate for a successful advertising campaign than kidney plasters. Yet the ad, showing a boy and girl sitting by the oceanside, with his arm encircling her waist and the words—"Feels Good On The Back"—immediately captured the public's imagination. The demand for reprints was overwhelming, and soon poster-size copies of

the ad were in countless drugstore windows. Amateur and professional artists began drawing hundreds of variations which were reprinted in the Company magazine. While no one knew what the girl in the ad looked like, she became everybody's favorite. During the war the photo and theme were used over and over to illustrate the confidence men and women in service had with a united country at their backs. The ad would run for an incredible thirty years, and despite periodic protests from fashion stylists, only once was the young lady's attire modernized. Even that change drew a flood of complaints from fans who wanted to keep her just as she was.

By now the Company's products had gained a strong position in international markets, and some ninety percent of all of the cotton gauze and bandages in use throughout the world were coming from JOHNSON & JOHNSON. To promote its international business, the Company distributed photos showing Red Cross products being carried by a camel in India, by dog sled in the Arctic, and in the basket of a hot air balloon in Ger-

many. Advertising in professional publications was more restrained, centering around the theme of an attractive nurse in a uniform with a Red Cross emblem on her shoulder, carrying various Red Cross brand products in her hand.

At home a mammoth sign was erected on the roof of one of the buildings close to the main line tracks of the Pennsylvania Railroad. It measured 102 feet across and was twenty feet high, with the JOHNSON & JOHNSON name in white lights and two huge flashing red crosses on either side. At night the sign could be seen for miles and soon it became a landmark for travelers, especially the thousands of railroad passengers who passed it every day enroute to and from New York. Later, slogans were added to the sign in support of various causes, such as war bond drives and food conservation programs.

"All the News That's
Fit to Print."

The New York Times

VOL. LXVI...NO. 21,623 ... NEW YORK, SATURDAY, APRIL 7, 1917.—EIGHTEEN PAGES.

PRESIDENT PROCLAIMS WAR; WARNS ALIE
91 GERMAN SHIPS SEIZED AND

By 1916 the war in Europe had been under way for two years and the demand by the Allied Armies for surgical dressings produced by JOHNSON & JOHNSON was staggering. No company in Europe had anywhere near the same production capacity, and in the United States it was significantly higher than all other competitors combined. Added to the war demand was the growing acceptance for the same products in American hospitals. Extra shifts were added, but the orders continued to pile up.

To meet the demand, a search began for a new source of textiles. On June 1, 1916, Chicopee Manufacturing Company of Chicopee Falls, Massachusetts, was acquired for $1 million in cash. Soon the entire output of Chicopee's spinning and weaving operations went to New Brunswick for finishing as surgical dressings and other medical supplies in support of the European war effort.

At first, the German aggression in Europe seemed distant to most Americans, many of whom were still clinging to Woodrow Wilson's promises of neutrality. That attitude took an abrupt turn on May 7, 1915, when German U-boats sank the British liner *Lusitania* off the coast of Ireland, with a loss of 1,198 lives, many of them vacationing Americans. To some a global war seemed imminent, but in November of 1916 voters re-elected Woodrow Wilson president on the strength of his slogan, "He Kept Us Out Of War." The headlines of campaign rhetoric were soon replaced by the appalling toll of new sinkings by the U-boats. On April 2, 1917, Congress declared war against Germany and General John J. "Black Jack" Pershing led the American Expeditionary Forces to battle.

In New Brunswick, the bandage machines began running day and night seven days a week to keep up with the demand, which now included all of the Allied Forces as well as military and civilian hospitals at home and many in Europe.

In increasing numbers men left their production line jobs to enter military service, and their places were taken by women, many of them entering the work force for the first time. But their lack of experience did not deter the Company from shattering all production records. When journalist and author Janet Stewart visited the Company to see the production output first hand, she wrote: "The war has forced this always busy factory to make machinery that can turn out in a given time one hundred times as much as the machinery in use before America went to war." While that estimate was high, it was a fact that production of gauze and adhesive plaster was now being counted in terms of "thousands of miles," and bandages in the "hundreds of millions."

Robert Johnson, now twenty-five, had advanced to a senior position in manufacturing. During the war he became vice president of manufacturing when the man holding that post became ill and was forced to resign.

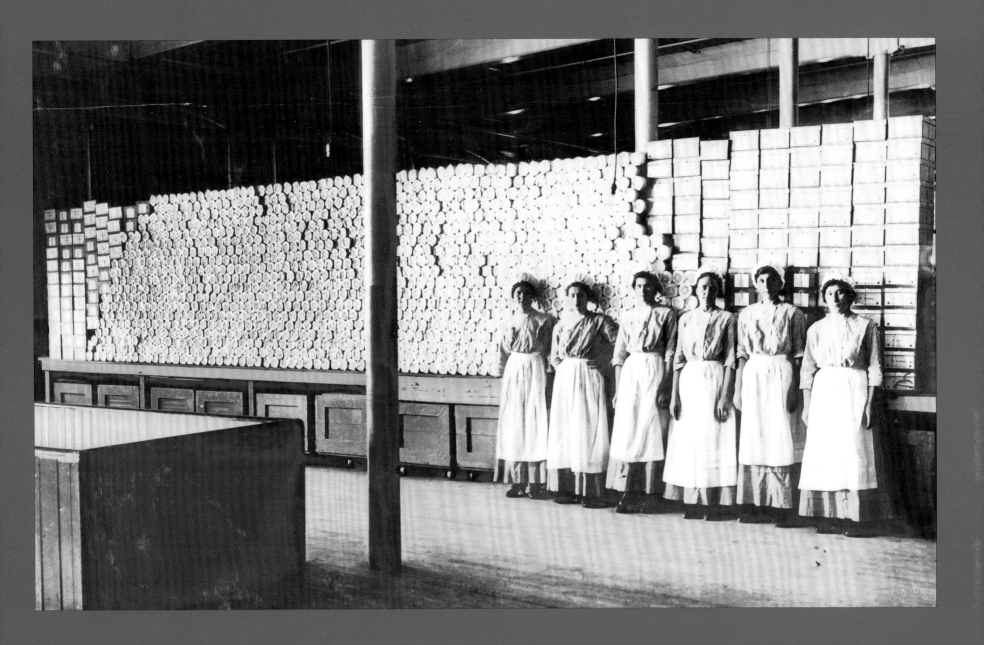

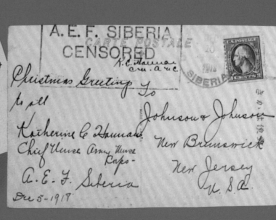

From Katherine C. Hannan C.N.
Army Nurse Corps
A.E.F. Siberia

Arrived early last week.
Had a fairly nice trip over.
Stopping 5 days in Japan. It
was a small town. We
were glad to see this place.
It is most wonderfull. I
shall tell you all about
it by letter later. Trust
you are well—

Kittie
Nov. 10 - 1918

A.E.F. SIBERIA
CENSORED
K.C. Hannan
Cn. A.N.C.

Christmas Greeting to
to all

Katherine C. Hannan
Chief Nurse Army Nurse
Corps—
A.E.F. Siberia
Dec 5 - 1918

Johnson & Johnson
New Brunswick
New Jersey
U.S.A.

Modern warfare presented new challenges to even the most gifted physicians. The noted French surgeon, Dr. Alexis Carrel, was so appalled at the high rate of amputations among the wounded due to infection that he began developing a new antiseptic system that later involved Fred Kilmer and his associates at JOHNSON & JOHNSON. Carrel found that deep wounds such as those inflicted by exploding shells healed better if kept constantly irrigated with an antiseptic solution. Working at his laboratory at Compiegne,

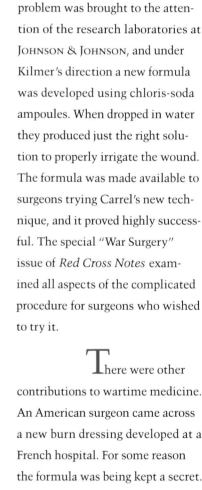

France, he devised an apparatus to irrigate wounds that used a solution developed by an English chemist. The formula called for the use of ordinary bleaching lime, which was found to be unstable and risky. This problem was brought to the attention of the research laboratories at JOHNSON & JOHNSON, and under Kilmer's direction a new formula was developed using chloris-soda ampoules. When dropped in water they produced just the right solution to properly irrigate the wound. The formula was made available to surgeons trying Carrel's new technique, and it proved highly successful. The special "War Surgery" issue of *Red Cross Notes* examined all aspects of the complicated procedure for surgeons who wished to try it.

There were other contributions to wartime medicine. An American surgeon came across a new burn dressing developed at a French hospital. For some reason the formula was being kept a secret. He obtained a sample and sent it to the Company's research laboratories, where in a short time an improved version was developed. It was called Redintol, a preparation of paraffin and resins with dissimi-

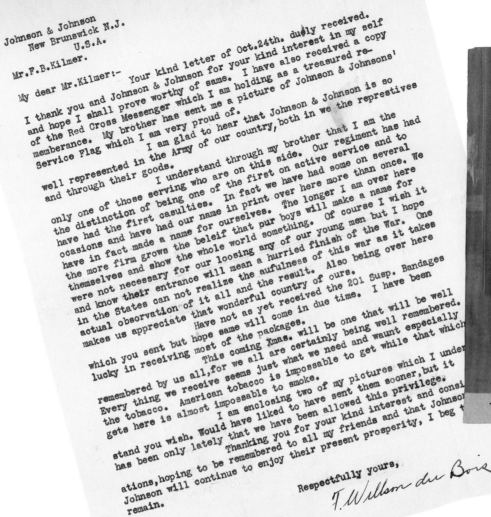

Johnson & Johnson
New Brunswick N.J.
U.S.A.

Mr.F.B.Kilmer.

My dear Mr.Kilmer:-
Your kind letter of Oct.24th. duely received.
I thank you and Johnson & Johnson for your kind interest in my self
and hope I shall prove worthy of same. I have also received a copy
of the Red Cross Messenger which I am holding as a treasured re-
memberance. My brother has sent me a picture of Johnson & Johnsons'
Service Flag which I am very proud of.
I am glad to hear that Johnson & Johnson is so
well represented in the Army of our country, both in we the represtives
and through their goods.
I understand through my brother that I am the
only one of those serving who are on this side. Our regiment has had
the distinction of being one of the first on active service and to
have had the first casulties. In fact we have had some on several
ocasions and have had our name in print over here more than once. We
have in fact made a name for ourselves. The longer I am over here
the more firm grows the beleif that pur boys will make a name for
themselves and show the whole world something. Of course I wish it
were not necessary for our loosing any of our young men but I hope
and know their entrance will mean a hurried finish of the War. One
in the States can not realize the aufulness of this war as it takes
actual obsorvation of it all and the result. Also being over here
makes us appreciate that wonderful country of ours.
Have not as yet received the 201 Susp. Bandages
which you sent but hope same will come in due time. I have been
lucky in receiving most of the packages.
This coming Xmas. will be one that will be well
remembered by us all,for we all are certainly being well remembered.
Every thing we receive seems just what we need and waunt especially
the tobacco. American tobacco is impossable to get while that which
gets here is almost impossable to smoke.
I am enclosing two of my pictures which I understand you wish. Would have liked to have sent them sooner,but it
has been only lately that we have been allowed this privilege.
Thanking you for your kind interest and consi-
ations,hoping to be remembered to all my friends and that Johnson
Johnson will continue to enjoy their present prosperity, I beg t
remain.

Respectfully yours,
F. Willam du Bois

Some where in France
F. Willam du Bois 1917

War Surgery Issue

Series VII   Number Nine

RED CROSS NOTES

PUBLISHED BY *Johnson + Johnson* NEW BRUNSWICK, N.J., U.S.A.
Copyright 1918, Johnson & Johnson

"SOMEWHERE IN FRANCE"

King George Frequently Visits the Field Hospitals, Speaks Words of Comfort and
Cheer to the Fallen Heroes and Pays Tribute to the Modern Science of Surgery

lar melting points. The ingredients were formed into brown bars resembling cakes of maple sugar. When applied to the wound site and covered with an air-excluding shell, the healing was remarkable.

Even in normal times Kilmer was a prodigious worker who could be found in his laboratories long into the night. But during the war he pushed himself mercilessly. "It is this way," he explained: "If there are one million men under arms at the front, that means that hospital supplies for twice that number must be ready."

A father figure to many of the younger employees, Kilmer began corresponding with a number of the men and women who went into service. He would send them notes of encouragement and print accounts of their experiences in company publications. Kilmer's own son, Joyce, the talented writer and poet, had enlisted in the Army and was serving on a battlefront in France. As a youth Joyce had grown up in New Brunswick and he had many friends among the long-time JOHNSON & JOHNSON employees. From time to time Joyce would pen a short article for a Company publication and the employees took great pride in his association with JOHNSON & JOHNSON.

Trees

I think that I shall never see
A poem lovely as a tree.

A tree whose hungry mouth is prest
Against the earth's sweet flowing breast;

A tree that looks at god all day
And lifts her leafy arms to pray;

A tree that may in Summer wear
A nest of robins in her hair;

Upon whose bosom snow has lain;
Who intimately lives with rain

Poems are made by fools like me
But only god can make a tree.

Joyce Kilmer

Mahwah, N. J.
May 7, 1915.

Joyce Kilmer's most famous poem, "Trees," was supposedly inspired by a spreading white oak tree that grew in New Brunswick. The sinking of the *Lusitania* jolted the sensitive author and he began writing about the nobility of war and the warrior's calling, so long as the cause was holy. It was not surprising to his friends when two weeks after the United States entered the war Joyce enlisted in the Army, saying that he was "a poet trying to be a soldier." He went overseas with the 165th Infantry Regiment, the famous "Fighting 69th," composed of a rambunctious group of Irish-Americans.

From battlefields in France, Kilmer wrote about his comrades with affection and understanding: "Say a prayer for them all, they're brave men and good, and splendid company." Late in July of 1918, along the banks of the Ourcq River an aide to Major "Wild Bill" Donovan was killed in action and

Kilmer, now a sergeant in the intelligence section, volunteered to replace him. He greatly admired Donovan's bold leadership, and on the morning of July 30 accompanied him on a scouting mission. The two separated for a short time, and when the major returned he found that Kilmer had been killed by enemy fire.

News of Joyce's death, at the age of thirty-one, moved swiftly through the regiment. His comrades gathered for a hasty service near the village of Seringes. Sergeant Alexander Woolcott, correspondent for *The New York Times*, wrote about it:

"They all knew his verse *(Rouge Bouquet)*. I found any number of men who had only to fish around in their tattered blouses to bring out the copy of a poem Kilmer wrote in memory of some of their number who were killed by a shell in March." To the refrain of a bugler's "Taps," the chaplain, Father Francis Duffy, read Kilmer's *Rouge Bouquet*:

*"In a wood they call the
Rouge Bouquet
There is a new-made grave today,
Built by never a spade or pick
Yet covered with earth
ten metres thick
There lie many fighting men,
Dead in their youthful prime,
Never to laugh nor love again
Nor taste the Summertime."*

They said, according to Woolcott, that tears streamed down the face of every man in the regiment. Some of the tears might well have been saved for Fred and Annie Kilmer, who had now lost their fourth and last child. Annie Kilmer devoted the rest of her life to perpetuating Joyce's memory by setting many of his poems to music.

In 1920 another of JOHNSON & JOHNSON's most famous products, the BAND-AID Brand Adhesive Bandage, was "discovered" quite by accident. Earle E. Dickson, a cotton mill employee, was distressed because his young bride, Josephine, was constantly cutting herself while working in the kitchen. Patiently Dickson bandaged her fingers but the accidents kept occurring. Finally, he decided to make a ready-to-use bandage that she could apply herself. Laying out a long strip of surgical tape he placed small pieces of gauze on it at intervals, and to keep the adhesive from sticking he covered it with a piece of textured cotton crinoline. Whenever Josephine wounded herself she cut a piece of the tape and gauze pad and used it as a bandage.

When Dickson mentioned his "invention" to a co-worker he was encouraged to inform his superintendent.

"The boys in the front office loved the concept," Dickson recalled. The first BAND-AID product was an adhesive strip two and a half inches wide. It could be cut into strips of any size and went on the market in 1921. Sales the first year were only $3,000. Salesmen would carry a scissors with them and make the rounds of doctors' offices and drugstores, snipping off pieces of the new bandage to demonstrate its versatility.

Machines were then designed to make individual BAND-AID adhesive bandages and in time they were being produced by the millions. It became the biggest selling product in the Company's history. Dickson was made a vice president as reward for his ingenuity, and Josephine's clumsiness in the kitchen became a legend.

Seward and Robert Johnson

In the aftermath of the war the Company's production levels remained high for a time as supplies of hospital and consumer products were replenished. It was apparent, however, that new growth opportunities would have to be found.

Robert Johnson had moved out of manufacturing and was now in sales and marketing, areas for which he had a natural affinity. Looking ahead he saw the need for the Company to develop strong international markets. "Sometime about 1921," he later wrote, "I determined that America was being forced to a policy of isolation and that our export business was about to be destroyed."

At the time there was a strong argument for isolation. Many Americans felt that the country had been drawn into the war needlessly, and had paid bitterly. The casualty toll had been staggering, and across the country memorials to the war dead were grim reminders of just how costly the conflict had been. The advocates of isolation were vocal: "Let Americans take care of America, and let the foreigners take care of the foreigners," they proclaimed.

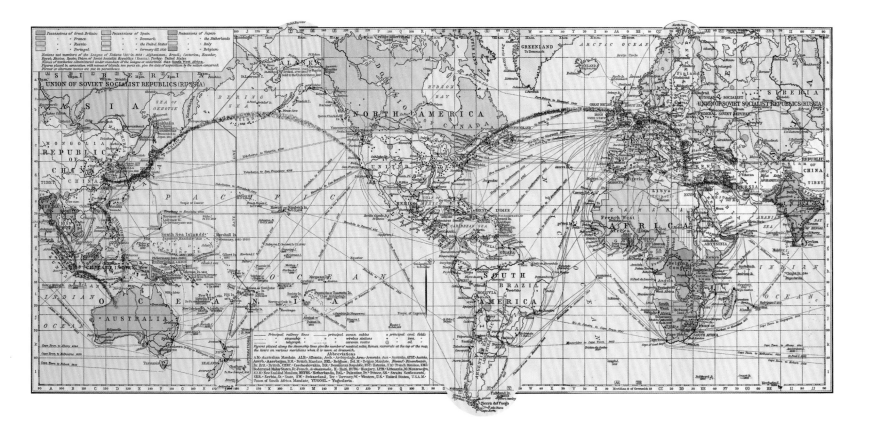

Political issues aside, the risks of expanding a business overseas were many and the rewards uncertain.

Johnson was virtually alone in believing that the Company should form international manufacturing operations. Others, including James Johnson, the President, favored expanding the existing network of sales agents and distributors. For over a year the issue was debated without resolution. Later Johnson recalled what happened next: "In the fall of 1922 my brother, Seward, and I asked the Board to approve a study of the British Empire. Our company needed first hand information about the chances of doing business in a vast and powerful family of nations spread all over the world. We could also get facts on some other nations, such as France, China and Japan."

Reluctantly, the Board agreed to the trip, though several members saw it as little more than a lark. "When permission was granted," Johnson wrote, "we started to plan what may have seemed like an easy, plushy tour. Actually, it didn't work out according to the travel folders."

After months of research on world business conditions, Johnson and his brother left New York October 1, 1923, aboard the *SS Olympia.* Over the next six months Johnson wrote thirty-six letters to the Company management, reporting on the potential of world markets he visited. He visited twelve countries, interviewing hundreds of businessmen, government officials, and knowledgeable people in the health field. By the time he returned the following spring he was more convinced than ever of the need to establish international manufacturing units, beginning with England. After much effort he persuaded the management to go along with his proposal, and in 1924 he personally supervised the opening of the plant at Slough, near London.

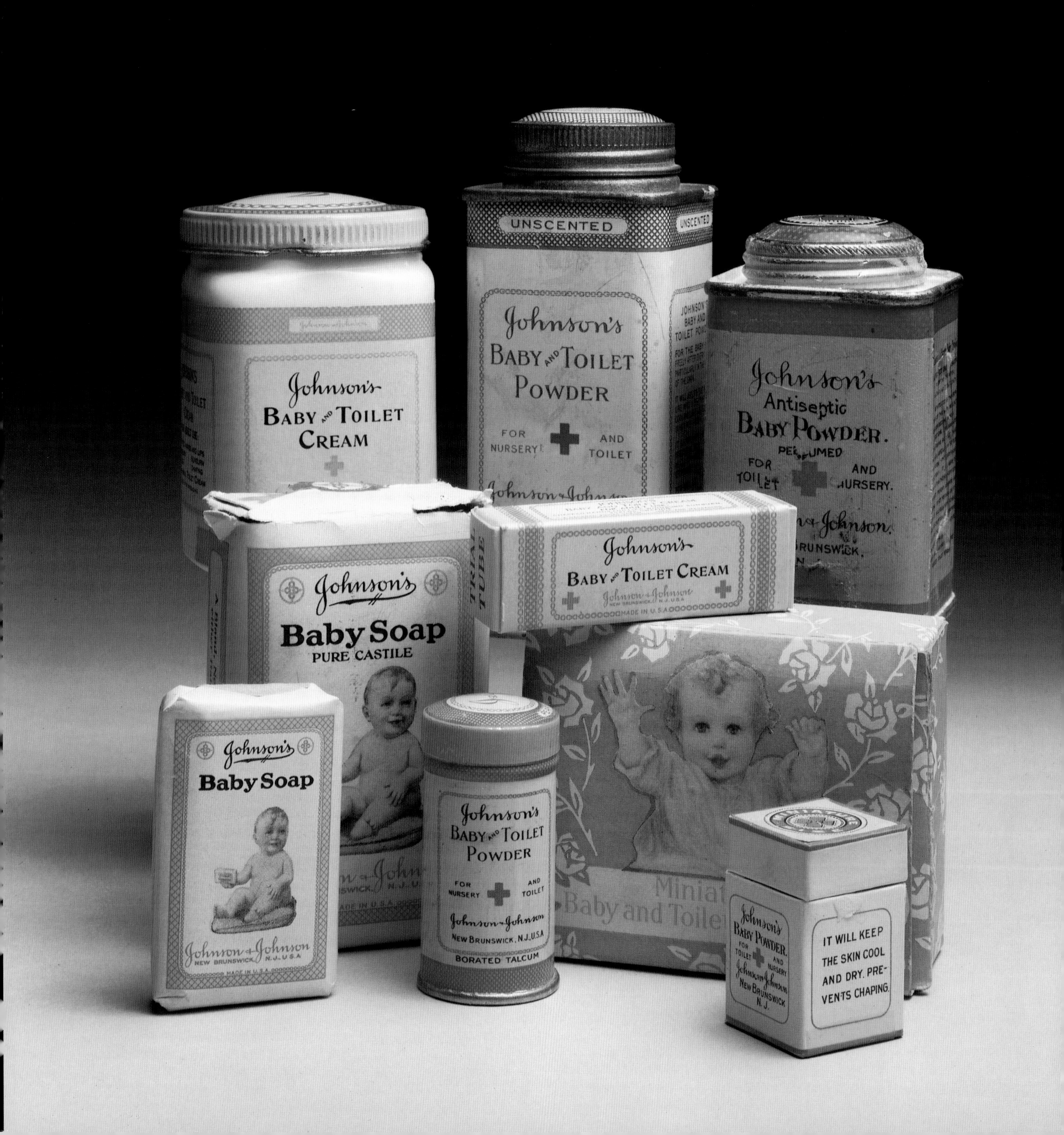
UNSCENTED
Johnson's
BABY AND TOILET
POWDER
FOR NURSERY
AND TOILET
Johnson's
BABY AND TOILET
CREAM
Johnson's
Antiseptic
BABY POWDER.
PERFUMED
FOR TOILET
AND NURSERY.
Johnson's
BABY AND TOILET CREAM
TRIAL TUBE
MADE IN U.S.A.
Johnson's
Baby Soap
PURE CASTILE
Johnson's
Baby Soap
Johnson & Johnson
NEW BRUNSWICK, N.J., U.S.A.
MADE IN U.S.A.
Johnson's
BABY AND TOILET
POWDER
FOR NURSERY
AND TOILET
Johnson & Johnson
NEW BRUNSWICK, N.J., U.S.A.
BORATED TALCUM
Johnson's
BABY POWDER.
FOR TOILET
AND NURSERY
Johnson & Johnson
NEW BRUNSWICK
N.J.
IT WILL KEEP
THE SKIN COOL
AND DRY. PRE-
VENTS CHAPING.

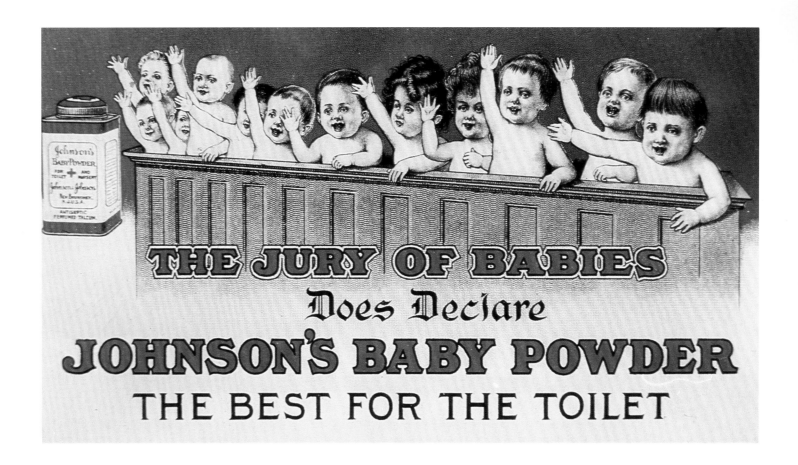

THE JURY OF BABIES
Does Declare
JOHNSON'S BABY POWDER
THE BEST FOR THE TOILET

No product ever did more to create a positive image for a company than did JOHNSON's Baby Powder. Mere mention of it stimulated pleasant memories of babies and motherhood, and its delicate scent became one of the most recognizable of all consumer products.

Sensing baby powder's great appeal, JOHNSON & JOHNSON began to build an entire business around products used in the nursery. Their success was rooted in the strength of the consumer acceptance that baby powder had gained. Some one hundred years later

JOHNSON's Baby Powder would still be demonstrating amazing vitality, strong sales, and the same positive reactions among consumers of all ages.

Though JOHNSON's Baby Powder had been on the market for close to thirty years, it was not until the years just after World War I that it made its real debut with vast numbers of American consumers. Advertising was in its heyday, and baby powder became the subject of the largest ad campaign in the Company's history. An array of smiling, cherubic babies was used in the four-color ads that appeared repeatedly in the major home magazines. The ads had such great appeal that they were enlarged into showcards for use in the display windows of thousands of

drugstores. Inside the stores, customers were greeted by countertop cards that read:

*YOUR BABY DESERVES
THE BEST
Your baby is our most particular
customer. Only the best
is good enough for the
health and happiness of the
little darling. Mothers
tell us they have confidence in
buying baby's needfuls
at our store.
By the way, are you using
JOHNSON's Toilet
and Baby Powder*

*BEST FOR BABY—
BEST FOR YOU.*

Owning their first automobiles enabled many American families to enjoy far greater mobility than ever before. Now they could range far beyond their corner druggists to shop for medications and sundries, from hair pins to school supplies. As a result, druggists were soon feeling the impact of reduced sales and customer traffic. Sensing an opportunity, JOHNSON & JOHNSON created the slogan "Your Druggist Is More Than a Merchant," and made it the theme of a national advertising campaign. It was soon picked up by druggists who started using the phrase in their own advertising. The popularity of the slogan grew with each new wave of advertising in which it was used. Then the editor of one eminent pharmaceutical journal refused to accept the advertising containing the slogan because, as he claimed, "Your Druggist Is More Than A Merchant" presented "an incomplete thought." Besides, he said, too many people were adding their own ending, "He is a bootlegger."

Debate over prohibition of alcoholic beverages was then raging throughout the country, so in the minds of some druggists it was a problem. The marketing department at JOHNSON & JOHNSON rose to the challenge and came up with a new phrase: "Your Druggist Is More Than a Merchant. Try The Drug Store First." That did it! The campaign went back into high gear. Pharmacy associations all over the country now adopted it as their official slogan. In Oklahoma druggists staged a parade and carried it on huge banners. In Texas druggists pooled their advertising budgets and used it in "truth" campaigns. Druggists in Louisiana and

Connecticut did the same. In Canada it was translated into French. It became popular in England, Australia, and South Africa, and on the Island of St. Kitts, where it was modified to "Your Chemist Is More Than a Merchant."

Kilmer estimated that the slogan appeared one billion times in advertising and promotions. "Is it any wonder that it has become a part of the language of the people?" he asked, somewhat in awe. For good measure, Kilmer elaborated on the theme with a series of tributes to druggists that appeared in JOHNSON & JOHNSON ads in the major journals of the day.

As Robert Johnson's experience in the business broadened, he assumed an even stronger role in management. He was maturing into a competent businessman and had earned the respect of his seniors. Those who felt otherwise were prudent enough to keep their thoughts to themselves, considering Johnson's position as the majority stockholder. In 1926 Johnson announced plans to build the world's most modern textile mill, and not surprisingly there was no opposition.

JOHNSON & JOHNSON had become a major producer of textile products, with the bulk of the output going into its surgical dressings. Since the days of the Industrial Revolution, textile mills had been bleak and dingy places to work, often with oppressive and unsafe working conditions. Most were concentrated in New England and the South, where wages were low and worker complaints went unheeded. The conditions in Johnson's own textile mills were less than ideal, in sharp contrast to the high standards that had been set in the Company's other factories. It was this marked difference that disturbed Johnson and compelled him to take action.

After a long search for a site, a beautiful tract of land was purchased near Gainesville, Georgia. In addition to the modern, one-story mill the Company announced that it would also construct a village for employees, with 200 modern homes, a school, churches and a medical facility. Those familiar with textile mills doubted Johnson's promise.

The site included the watershed of the Chatahoochee River to ensure a pure water supply for the spinning and weaving operations. When construction was completed, the sprawling mill had both technical excellence and an aesthetic beauty never before seen in the textile industry. One visiting writer declared: "The plant in Georgia is as nearly perfect as a modern cotton mill could be." Even before it was completed it

became a showplace that attracted factory and mill designers from all over the world.

In Chicopee Village, as it came to be known, thirty-one variations of modern brick homes were built with three, four, and five bedrooms. They were laid out on gracefully curved, attractively landscaped streets, with power lines underground. They were among the first homes in Northeast Georgia to have indoor plumbing, electricity and hot water. The mill and the homes changed the lives of those fortunate enough to obtain a job and live there. Many proclaimed it the most advanced step ever taken in the textile industry.

To celebrate the opening of the new mill local businessmen organized a barbecue for hundreds of employees and area residents. They gave Johnson a silver bowl and pitcher, and his reply was as much a reminder to his own management as it was a thank you: "May we conduct ourselves that we shall continue to merit the good will and confidence of the citizens of Hall County."

In the years ahead Johnson would carry out his "Factories Can Be Beautiful" philosophy by building more than a hundred attractive and efficient plants and office buildings. In 1926 the new Chicopee mill was unique.

We can conceive of no higher endeavor than the conscientious preparation for the medical and nursing professions of the means for combating the ills of humanity ~ *Johnson & Johnson*

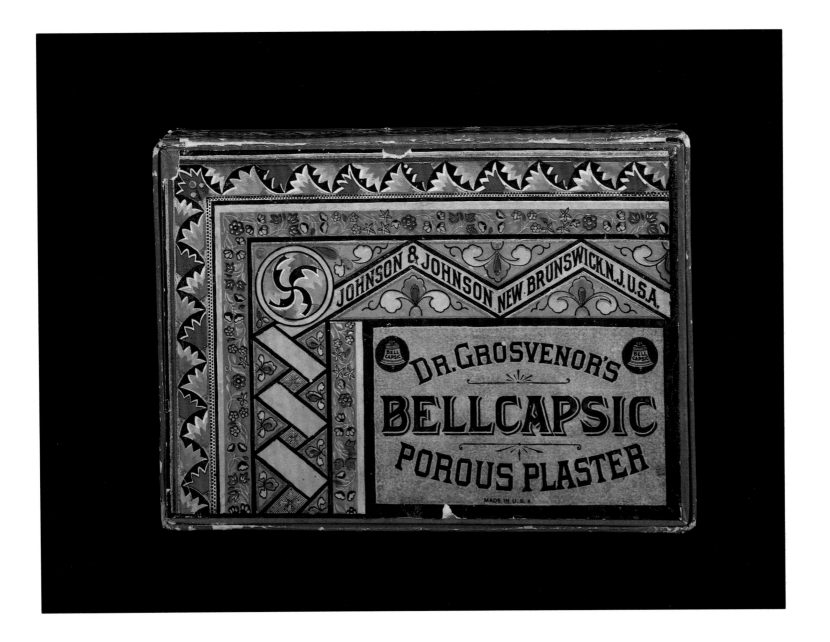

    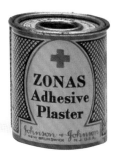

From the earliest days of medicine, physicians had tried to find new ways to use adhesives to promote healing. The adhesive mass was messy, time-consuming, and frustrating. Greek physicians used olive oil mixed with lead oxide, and a later formula contained rosin and yellow beeswax. But it wasn't until the middle of the 19th Century and the addition of India rubber that adhesive tape was introduced to medical care. In 1887 the Johnson brothers introduced the most improved adhesive tape on the market. They spread the adhesive mass on a strong cloth backing and wound the tape on a cylindrical tin spool. It was a devilish product to manufacture. When the mixture wasn't just right and the heat wasn't applied properly the whole batch had to be thrown out. Even the good tape presented problems. If it wouldn't stick properly it had to be heated over a flame; and when it stuck too much, patients suffered when it was removed. Despite these inconsistencies, JOHNSON's Adhesive Tape gained wide acceptance. Physicians used it in countless ways, from taping sprained ankles to holding surgical dressings in place. And consumers kept finding new uses for adhesive tape, from holding toupees and wigs in place to using it for makeshift patches.

As popular as they were, the early tapes often caused skin irritation. The next major advance, one that revolutionized the adhesive tape business, came in 1899 when JOHNSON & JOHNSON added zinc oxide to the formula. This gave the tape much stronger sticking qualities and sharply reduced skin irritation. With these improvements, the Company was well on its way to capturing the adhesive tape market. By 1910 there were dozens of different types of JOHNSON's Adhesive Tapes, plain or porous, and with various backings in more than a hundred combinations of length and width. The roll rack for use in hospitals was introduced in 1927, and gave the physician and nurse a choice of tapes on one long roll that fitted on a wall rack. Next came waterproof tape, and with each innovation the manufacturing process presented a greater challenge. But the market remained loyal to the Red Cross brand.

As the carefree Roaring Twenties drew to a close, the first dark clouds of the Great Depression began forming over the nation like a gathering storm. Herbert Hoover was elected president in 1928 because voters had believed his campaign rhetoric: "We in America today are nearer to the final triumph over poverty than ever before in the history of our land." Robert Johnson attended the Republican National Convention in Kansas City as an alternate delegate and strong Hoover supporter. But later that summer, when industrial production and consumer spending began to lag, Johnson became gravely concerned and urged his management to curtail all major spending.

Despite the warning signs, investors continued to pour huge amounts of money into the stock market. On Thursday, October 29, — Black Thursday, as it became known — the market collapsed after the most disastrous day in its history. The decline in stock values reached $40 billion, and the nation was in the grips of the Great Depression. Unemployment soared to twenty-five percent and millions of the jobless lined up at soup kitchens for food to sustain themselves.

On February 4, 1930, Johnson became vice president and general manager. During the early months of the Depression many companies failed. Faced by the mounting threats to the business, Johnson shortened work shifts, eliminated Saturday work, and asked production employees to take three-day weekends twice a month. He also reduced the salaries of all senior executives, including his own, by fifteen percent. These cutbacks were mild compared with measures being taken at other companies, and all during the Depression no jobs were lost at JOHNSON & JOHNSON. To the contrary, Johnson extended the bonus system to include salesmen, based on a new incentive plan. While offering encouragement to his workers, he had sharp criticism for his Board of Directors, all of whom were members of management: "I am anxious that this Board begin to function in some way that will be of use to JOHNSON & JOHNSON, and we would welcome any recommendations toward that end. As a body for disseminating information it is already useful, but for an intelligent discussion of a major problem it does not disclose its value. The fault for this may rest with the stockholders and, if so, recommendations will be in order." The reference to "stockholders," of course, was to himself and others in senior management.

WONDERFUL MOTHER

To be a Mother is to be among the greatest artists of the world. A tiny will, a tiny mind, even the threads of a Future are in her hands. What will she build with them?

"I had a wonderful mother," said Lincoln. "All that I am I owe to her."

If greatness is a gift, the greatest gift a baby can have is a wonderful mother —a mother who knows that hours and hours of restful sleep are essential to baby's future.

Does it seem odd that a mere "baby powder advertisement" should be so serious? Perhaps baby powder isn't so mere after all.

Do you realize that Johnson's Baby Powder was the suggestion of a famous physician who knew that skin comfort is the surest path to sounder sleep? And that it is made especially for babies in laboratories that prepare hundreds of articles for the medical profession?

The difference between Johnson's Baby Powder and ordinary talcums appeals to a mother.

Johnson's Baby Powder

Best for baby-Best for you

In the spring of 1932 Robert Johnson became President of JOHNSON & JOHNSON, succeeding his uncle, James, who was then seventy-six. James had not been active in the business for many years due to failing health. Even so, in deference to his role as a co-founder of the Company, he was permitted to retain the title of President and continue as a member of the Board of Directors. But when he received notice that he would henceforth be listed as a "pensioner" with benefits of $2,500 a year instead of the "reduced salary" he had been receiving, James became rankled. He promptly resigned, not only as President and director but also, as he put it, as "pensioner."

The early years of Robert Johnson's presidency found

FINAL NEWS
EDITION

World

Market in Panic as Stocks Are Dumped in 12,894,600 Share Day; Bankers Halt It

Outside J. P. Morgan & Co.'s

the Company battling to survive the Depression. Just prior to the economic collapse, annual sales reached $20 million for the first time, but the next four years saw a modest decline.

In the early 1930s, Johnson continued to gain prominence as an industrialist with a creative approach to running a business. He also became a public figure. A decade earlier he had served as mayor of Highland Park, his home community, and later became involved in state and national politics, but in a behind-the-scenes role. In the presidential campaign of 1932 Herbert Hoover faced a newcomer to the national political scene, Franklin D. Roosevelt. It was during this period that Johnson, whose politics rode the entire sweep of the pendulum from conservative to liberal, became enamored of some of Roosevelt's views.

Roosevelt defeated Hoover in a landslide. Six weeks before he was inaugurated in 1933 he received a letter from Johnson outlining a plan for the nation's economic recovery, calling for a Federal law increasing wages and a reduction of hours in the work week. Coming as it did at a time when most employers were strug-

gling to meet their payrolls, the plan received wide attention in the press and some acclaim. One paper editorialized: "Many 'big men' have realized this necessity (higher wages), but Mr. Johnson is one of the few to come out publicly, not only in favor but in agitation for it." Word came from Roosevelt that he would be considering Johnson's proposals after he took office. An anxious nation was awaiting the president-elect's own plan for economic recovery, which turned out to be the New Deal. No action was taken on Johnson's proposals, but in June he gave his own employees a five percent pay increase, noting

that he hoped it would set a trend for the rest of the industry. Few companies followed his example.

As President, Johnson exerted a strong influence on the direction of the business, putting greater emphasis on the advertising and marketing of consumer products, and on the research and development of new products. He stressed product quality and better packaging. Like his father, he had the capacity to rally people toward a goal, and when diplomacy didn't work he used more persuasive methods. There was little doubt who was in charge.

SURGICAL DRESSING EXPERT TO VISIT HERE IN AUTO-GYRO

Robert Wood Johnson, general manager of Johnson & Johnson, surgical dressing firm, and the auto-gyro in which he is making a tour of the Middlewest, studying economic and business conditions.

Employing an auto-gyro to speed his tour, Robert Wood Johnson, general manager of the surgical dressing firm of Johnson & Johnson, New Brunswick, N. J., is due in Wichita this week.

Robert Johnson was an interesting, sometimes fascinating combination of astute businessman, idealist, patriot and man about town. He made mistakes, but rarely admitted them. He enjoyed his wealth to the fullest, but was often self-conscious about it. In later years he would not bring his most expensive car, a Rolls Royce, near the plant in New Brunswick, preferring instead to be dropped off several blocks away. Everyone knew, of course, that he owned the car, but flaunting it bothered him. He and his first wife, Elizabeth, had been divorced. Now, in the early 1930s, he lived with his second wife, fashion model Maggie Shea, at Morven in Princeton, New Jersey. The historic mansion was later to serve as the official home of New Jersey governors.

Growing up in New Brunswick as the richest young man in town, Johnson raised the eyebrows of his elders with his hell-raising. Some swore he would fail. They later credited his first marriage and the birth of his son, Robert, with helping to put his life back on track. But Johnson did not conform for very long. He was restless and, many said, ambitious to achieve goals beyond what life in New Brunswick offered him. He was also unconventional in many ways, and often unpredictable. He had a quick mind and a persuasive manner. He was highly opinionated and a staunch advocate of his fresh ideas, even after some of them went sour on him. There was one point on which both his admirers and critics could agree: he was different. He was also very generous. Just before Christmas in 1936 Johnson took 12,000 shares of JOHNSON & JOHNSON stock that he personally owned and used it to form the Johnson New Brunswick Foundation. Eventually this became The Robert Wood Johnson Foundation, one of the most influential forces in the nation for improved health care.

St. Peter's Hospital

The Foundation's early mission was to help the people of New Brunswick through the Depression. The funds were used to feed and clothe children, straighten their teeth, and give a dedicated policeman and father of eight a down payment on a house. Once, a trustee of the Foundation suggested consulting a lawyer about the legitimacy of a particular grant, and Johnson replied: "Well, let's go ahead with it and if we get in trouble then we'll call in the legal talent." Scores of young men and women from the city and its environs were given funds to attend medical, dental, and nursing schools, and few ever knew who their benefactor was. Johnson ran the Foundation in its early years according to his own views on philanthropy, helping those he felt were most in need of help. His generosity was often a problem for his associates on the Foundation Board. "You had to watch him or he would give the store away," one recalled.

Later the scope of the Foundation was broadened to include as major beneficiaries the two local hospitals, Middlesex and St. Peter's, and numerous other area charities. Johnson had become a "student" of hospital management, constantly looking for new ways to improve patient care and the business aspects of running the institution. His first gift to Middlesex was the hospital's first office typewriter some twenty years earlier. Later, the gifts would total in the millions of dollars.

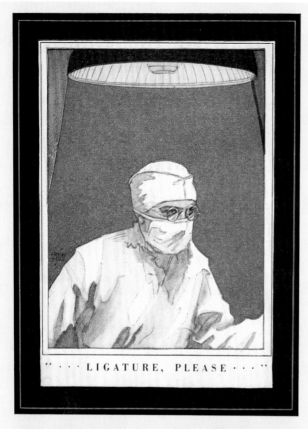

ETHICON

THE NEW NON-BOILABLE
CATGUT SUTURE

"···LIGATURE, PLEASE···"

Despite the adverse impact of the Depression, the Company's constantly expanding product line continued to gain favor with consumers. In 1934 a large manufacturing plant was opened in Chicago, the first major domestic facility outside of New Brunswick. The Chicago plant was another reflection of Johnson's strong belief in the philosophy of decentralizing the business into smaller, manageable units. He once recalled the incident that convinced him of the merits of decentralization. It seems that an improved formula had been introduced for making plaster products, but some annoying problems had developed in the early production runs. Johnson was determined to find the cause, so he called a meeting of all those who had any responsibility for producing the new adhesives. When seventeen people filed into his office, Johnson was dismayed. "I now know what the problem is," he told them, "too many people are involved." "The meeting is over," he said, ending it before it even began. Later he assigned one person the responsibility for finding and correcting the problem.

From then on, Johnson was convinced that the best way to run a business was to decentralize it, and this concept evolved into what became known as the JOHNSON & JOHNSON Family of Companies.

Another reason for Johnson's belief in independent units was the human factor. He once explained this in an article in the *Saturday Evening Post*: "Workers need recognition and appreciation," he wrote. "The need to be esteemed in terms of the human equation as well as the production chart." Smaller

operations, where more people could be recognized and rewarded, were his answer.

Over time, Johnson became the foremost disciple of decentralized management and his company one of the best examples of it. There was no set formula for accomplishing this, and it came about in various ways. From the Company's earliest days sutures were a part of the product line. In 1918 that business was expanded with the acquisition of the firm of Van Horn and Sawtell. Then in 1921 the Johnson Suture Corporation was formed, and out of it grew a line of sutures known as ETHICON. When that business grew large it became an affiliate company, Ethicon, Inc.

Other affiliates had their origins in the Company's research laboratories. In the late 1920s Dr. Gustave Mathey succeeded Fred Kilmer as head of research, and it was his laboratory discoveries that led the Company into the field of family planning and the formation of the Ortho Pharmaceutical Corporation.

The same principles were applied to the management of the rapidly expanding global business. New product lines were first placed with agents and, when the business grew to a point where it could sustain itself, new international affiliates were formed. The Company in Canada dated back to 1919; the one in Great Britain was formed in 1925, and these were followed by South Africa in 1930, Mexico and Australia in 1931, and Brazil and Argentina in 1937.

Modess

—SO INFINITELY FINER

Until you try it, such soft comfort seems beyond belief

You'll be delighted to discover at last a sanitary napkin of superlative softness and comfort. Modess is so infinitely finer in every way—so free from chafing—so safe—that you are certain to be enthusiastic in your preference.

The center or filler is unlike that of the ordinary napkin. It is not in stiff layers with square edges but is a soft, yielding mass like fluffy cotton which form makes it more highly absorbent. This filler is an entirely new substance invented by Johnson & Johnson. It disintegrates instantly when flushed away. Modess has smoothly rounded sides that cannot chafe.

The Johnson & Johnson gauze is specially softened and then for added comfort is cushioned with a film of cotton, giving a velvety softness. As a further protection, the soft back is rendered resistant to moisture by a method unknown to others.

The easiest and quickest way to learn how much better is Modess is to buy a box at your drug or department store, but we shall be glad to mail one Modess for you to examine. Just fill out the coupon below.

Johnson & Johnson
NEW BRUNSWICK, N. J., U. S. A.

**One Modess free
for examination**

Johnson & Johnson, New Brunswick, New Jersey   Dept. 14

I would like to receive one free Modess to examine carefully.

Name .... Address ....

Until a few weeks before his death in 1934, at the age of eighty-three, Fred Kilmer visited the Company almost every day. JOHNSON & JOHNSON had been the focal point of his life for forty-five years, and by his own choice he never retired. He came and went as he pleased, stopping in at the research laboratories or spending long hours in the archives he had set up to trace the history of the Company's trademarks and product development. Upon his death, *American Druggist* magazine described Kilmer as "…one of the most fascinating individuals American Pharmacy has given to the world." There were no words to describe what his presence had meant to the success of JOHNSON & JOHNSON.

The close relationship that he had helped develop over the years with druggists smoothed the way for the introduction of many new products, perhaps none as sensitive as MODESS sanitary

protection products for women. By 1933 sales were sufficient to warrant the formation of a new entity, the Modess Corporation, later to become Personal Products. The new company soon became a success despite a near calamitous beginning. Sales offices had been rented at 500 Fifth Avenue, New York, and to gain the attention of the drug trade a special two-for-one offer was widely advertised. Within days, even before the furniture arrived, there were ten bulging mail sacks of orders. "We decided to sort the orders alphabetically," a Modess executive recalled, "so we got a bunch of empty cartons, and by midnight we finally completed the job." Returning the next morning, they were horrified to find that the janitor, thinking the cartons of orders were waste paper, had thrown them out.

Robert Johnson's ultimate goal, which he later achieved, was to provide inexpensive sanitary protection pads to millions of women worldwide who never had access to them. He considered it undignified for women to have to resort to makeshift methods to meet these needs, and was especially determined to bring sanitary protection products to women in underdeveloped countries.

The New York Times.

LATE CITY EDITION
Cloudy followed by clearing and colder today. Tomorrow fair and moderately cold.
Temperature Yesterday—Max., 44; Min., 25

VOL. XCI. No. 30,635.   Entered as Second-Class Matter, Postoffice, New York, N. Y.   NEW YORK, TUESDAY, DECEMBER 9, 1941.   Copyright, 1941, by The New York Times Company.   THREE CENTS NEW YORK CITY and Vicinity

U. S. DECLARES WAR, PACIFIC BATTLE WIDENS; MANILA AREA BOMBED; 1,500 DEAD IN HAWAII; HOSTILE PLANES SIGHTED AT SAN FRANCISCO

TURN BACK TO SEA | Philippines Pounded

The attack on Pearl Harbor on December 7, 1941, sent the nation into a frenzy of wartime activity. People who worked on production lines equated patriotism with output and, the more important that products were to the war effort, the greater the sense of urgency to produce them in ever-increasing quantities. Both the U.S. and the Allied Forces had a pressing need for the array of medical and hospital products produced by JOHNSON & JOHNSON. In a short time all of the production records ever established by the Company were being broken. In addition, JOHNSON & JOHNSON was called upon to harness its management and production skills in several new and totally unfamiliar areas: gas masks and artillery shells.

Shortly after the war began, Johnson entered the Army with the rank of colonel and was assigned to the Ordnance Department to use his business skills in the procurement of war materials. Mobilizing small business firms into the mainstream of the war effort had become a national concern. Fewer than a hundred of the larger companies had seventy per-

cent of all war contracts while 10,000 small business firms languished. They were further threatened by sharp cutbacks in the production of civilian goods and tight controls on the availability of raw materials. The danger was that small business, which in peacetime was the backbone of the national economy, was doomed to systematic bankruptcy. To save small business from this fate, President Franklin D. Roosevelt named Johnson chairman of the Smaller War Plants Corporation and boosted his Army rank to brigadier general.

In Washington, as elsewhere, Johnson had established a reputation for being what the press called "industry's rebel." It was well earned. He had campaigned tirelessly for higher pay, shorter hours, and minimum wage laws, and in doing so had irked Congress and his peers in big business. At the same time, he became a folk hero of the working class. The press took every opportunity to fan

the controversy, which Johnson kept fueling with an endless supply of acerbic quotes to newsmen.

This set the stage for Johnson's stormy year in Washington. There he took on another adversary, the Army brass in the Pentagon. While he managed to divert substantial war work to small business, it was a struggle every step of the way, ending when illness forced him to return to civilian life. Before leaving the Capital in the fall of 1943 he fired a parting shot, delivered by way of Walter Winchell's nationally syndicated column. "Washington is a magnet for mediocrity," Johnson said tartly.

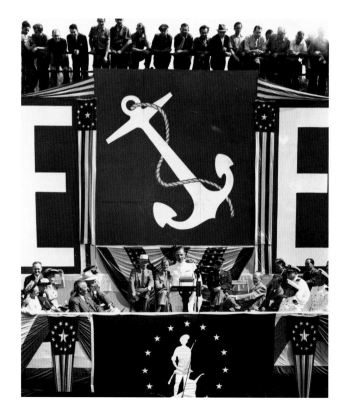

Public Patriotism at High Pitch
As Plants Hum with War Work

NEW BRUNSKICK, N. J. — If the phantoms of the founders of
this old city still hover in the hills around it, they must feel at home today. For New Brunswick, which sprung into national importance
first war for freedom, is swinging into the highest phase
ment as the latest war for liberty moves to

Over on the plains of Stelton,
a few miles from the city center,
Camp Kilmer, named for Joyce
Kilmer, the poet-patriot who
d here, is operating on th
here the cattle

rangements in the natio
the combination of
functions with

For the second time in twenty-five years the United States was plunged into a World War, and JOHNSON & JOHNSON's production of medical products was again put to a severe test. Only this time the "call to duty" went far beyond the making of bandages: it included gas masks, artillery shells, aircraft parts and large quantities of camouflage material. Most of these assignments were undertaken without profit. These wartime activities were summarized in the Company's 1945 annual report.

Johnson&Johnson and

THE ARMY-NAVY "E" flag which flies over the plants of Johnson & Johnson symbolizes the company's war efforts.

We are proud not alone of our war record and of the work of our employees, but also of the fact that this was the third time in the history of Johnson&Johnson that it was privileged to produce vitally needed war products for our nation's armed services. In both the Spanish-American War and in World War I, Johnson & Johnson provided surgical dressings for our forces.

The scope of World War II was such that Johnson & Johnson materiel, employed by our armed services, was so broad that to do other than high-light it would require more space than is here available.

Johnson & Johnson's production of gauze bandages for World War II, for example, was enough to supply the civilian requirements of the United States for approximately four years. It also produced many millions of yards of surgical gauze and crinoline. In addition, its output of war goods included millions of Plaster of Paris bandages, surgical sutures, "Band-Aids," surgical sponges, supporters, spools of adhesive, and toothbrushes.

Many other divisions of the company participated in the war effort. A Johnson & Johnson plant in Chicago was one of the few to produce gas masks for use of the armed forces. Unlike civilian gas masks, they were designed to meet all combat conditions. The gas mask factory, the first of our war plants, achieved the record of having the lowest production cost of all gas mask plants in the country.

At Illiopolis, Illinois, the company built a 10,000-acre plant within nine months designed to produce annually fifty million units of thirteen different kinds of shells varying in size from twenty to ninety millimeters.

the war effort

In Milltown, New Jersey, the Industrial Tape Corporation plant was one of the largest suppliers of industrial tape for the armed forces. These pressure-sensitive tapes, easy to handle and versatile in use, saved valuable time in manufacturing and packaging war materials. A wide variety of tapes to serve a multitude of particular purposes were made for the aviation industry alone. Actually hundreds of thousands of miles of special waterproof tapes were used on tanks, planes, and ammunition destined for overseas.

The versatility of Johnson & Johnson to meet the demands of war was exemplified in the Atlantic Diesel Corporation. This subsidiary produced large quantities of various precision equipment including hydraulic mechanisms for bomb bay doors, landing gear, and wing hinges, as well as torpedo parts, radar equipment, and rockets for Navy planes.

The Chicopee Manufacturing Company was the largest producer of plastic screenings for tents, huts, inner soles, and targets. This product, known as LUMITE. is not affected by humid salt air and was developed primarily to protect our forces in the South Pacific Bases. Besides being a principal supplier of gauze for processing into surgical dressings, Chicopee was the only supplier of unwoven cotton camouflage material used during the war.

TANTALUM, a metallic element fostered by the Ethicon Suture Laboratories, has proved to be one of the most dramatic surgical developments of the war. Ideal for head injuries, during the operation the surgeon can shape it, by hand and without heating, to fit the contours of the skull, and, further, it does not create tissue irritation. Of added importance, it can be drawn to a thread finer than a human hair, making it invaluable in repairing severed nerves as well as for general suture use. Significantly, it has been called the nearest thing to a "perfect metal" for surgery.

While we, of Johnson & Johnson, feel within ourselves that ours was an important war contribution, we are content to say, "We also served."

Our Credo

WE BELIEVE THAT OUR FIRST RESPONSIBILITY IS TO THE DOCTORS, NURSES, HOSPITALS,
MOTHERS, AND ALL OTHERS WHO USE OUR PRODUCTS.
OUR PRODUCTS MUST ALWAYS BE OF THE HIGHEST QUALITY.
WE MUST CONSTANTLY STRIVE TO REDUCE THE COST OF THESE PRODUCTS.
OUR ORDERS MUST BE PROMPTLY AND ACCURATELY FILLED.
OUR DEALERS MUST MAKE A FAIR PROFIT.

OUR SECOND RESPONSIBILITY IS TO THOSE WHO WORK WITH US —
THE MEN AND WOMEN IN OUR PLANTS AND OFFICES.
THEY MUST HAVE A SENSE OF SECURITY IN THEIR JOBS.
WAGES MUST BE FAIR AND ADEQUATE,
MANAGEMENT JUST, HOURS REASONABLE, AND WORKING CONDITIONS CLEAN AND ORDERLY.
EMPLOYEES SHOULD HAVE AN ORGANIZED SYSTEM FOR SUGGESTIONS AND COMPLAINTS.
SUPERVISORS AND DEPARTMENT HEADS MUST BE QUALIFIED AND FAIR MINDED.
THERE MUST BE OPPORTUNITY FOR ADVANCEMENT — FOR THOSE QUALIFIED
AND EACH PERSON MUST BE CONSIDERED AN INDIVIDUAL
STANDING ON HIS OWN DIGNITY AND MERIT.

OUR THIRD RESPONSIBILITY IS TO OUR MANAGEMENT.
OUR EXECUTIVES MUST BE PERSONS OF TALENT, EDUCATION, EXPERIENCE AND ABILITY.
THEY MUST BE PERSONS OF COMMON SENSE AND FULL UNDERSTANDING.

OUR FOURTH RESPONSIBILITY IS TO THE COMMUNITIES IN WHICH WE LIVE.
WE MUST BE A GOOD CITIZEN — SUPPORT GOOD WORKS AND CHARITY,
AND BEAR OUR FAIR SHARE OF TAXES.
WE MUST MAINTAIN IN GOOD ORDER THE PROPERTY WE ARE PRIVILEGED TO USE.
WE MUST PARTICIPATE IN PROMOTION OF CIVIC IMPROVEMENT,
HEALTH, EDUCATION AND GOOD GOVERNMENT,
AND ACQUAINT THE COMMUNITY WITH OUR ACTIVITIES.

OUR FIFTH AND LAST RESPONSIBILITY IS TO OUR STOCKHOLDERS.
BUSINESS MUST MAKE A SOUND PROFIT.
RESERVES MUST BE CREATED, RESEARCH MUST BE CARRIED ON,
ADVENTUROUS PROGRAMS DEVELOPED, AND MISTAKES PAID FOR.
ADVERSE TIMES MUST BE PROVIDED FOR, ADEQUATE TAXES PAID, NEW MACHINES PURCHASED,
NEW PLANTS BUILT, NEW PRODUCTS LAUNCHED, AND NEW SALES PLANS DEVELOPED.
WE MUST EXPERIMENT WITH NEW IDEAS.
WHEN THESE THINGS HAVE BEEN DONE THE STOCKHOLDER SHOULD RECEIVE A FAIR RETURN.
WE ARE DETERMINED WITH THE HELP OF GOD'S GRACE,
TO FULFILL THESE OBLIGATIONS TO THE BEST OF OUR ABILITY.

Johnson & Johnson

Beginning with Robert Johnson's rise as a young business executive, he repeatedly demonstrated his great concern for management's obligations to its employees. Like his father and uncle who headed the Company before him, he also held strong convictions about the link between product quality and the continuing success of JOHNSON & JOHNSON. In 1935, during the depths of the Great Depression, Johnson began to expand his views to include the responsibilities that he felt business had to society. In a message sent to the nation's leading businessmen, in a pamphlet he titled *Try Reality*, Johnson called for reforms in wages, hours and taxation. He also asked businessmen to embrace what he called "a new industrial philosophy." He described it in this way:

"Out of the suffering of the past few years has been born a public knowledge and conviction that industry only has the right to succeed where it performs a real economic service and is a true social asset. Such permanent success is possible only through the application of an industrial philosophy of enlightened self-interest. It is to the enlightened self-interest of modern industry to realize that its service to its *customers* comes first, its service to its *employees* and *management* second, and its service to its *stockholders* last. It is to the enlightened self-interest of industry to accept and fulfill its full share of social responsibility."

There was little response to Johnson's appeal, but eight years later, in 1943, he used the same four responsibilities—to customers, employees, management and stockholders—as the cornerstone of the Credo he wrote and put in place at Johnson & Johnson. It became a day-to-day management philosophy that he presided over zealously. Later Johnson added a fifth responsibility, to the community, and the Credo became widely acclaimed for its innovative approach to running a business. At the time business had not yet dealt broadly with the concept of social responsibility, but would in the years to come. While Johnson's Credo was not the first of its kind, it became one of the best known and the model for many others.

An important aspect of Johnson's philosophy was the connection he made between a business being socially responsible and its success. He explained this best in a preamble that later accompanied a modified version of his Credo:

"American institutions, both public and private, exist because the people want them, believe in them, or at least are willing to tolerate them. The day has passed when business was a private matter—if it ever really was. In a business society, every act of business has social consequences and may arouse public interest. Every time business hires, builds, sells or buys, it is acting for the American people as well as for itself, and it must be prepared to accept full responsibility for its acts…"

Some four decades later, Johnson's business philosophy would be put to its severest test when the company was confronted by the two TYLENOL crises. As it turned out, the Credo pointed the way to the responsible handling of those tragic events.

Johnson wrote about his wealth of ideas on business management in various national magazines. Soon his reputation as an outspoken business leader grew. As unionism gained strength he urged management to put greater emphasis on human relations and the dignity of the individual. He led a group of fifty labor, business and religious leaders and educators in a two-year study that resulted in a widely acclaimed report on "Human Relations in Modern Business." The *Harvard Business Review* called it a "Magna Carta for Business." Johnson initiated programs to encourage his employees to participate in politics and government service, and used his own company as his laboratory for the development of his many creative ideas for making business more responsible.

One of Johnson's most significant contributions to advanced business thinking was his book *Or Forfeit Freedom*, published in 1947. It was a frank essay on why business had lost so much public confidence and why there was so much management-labor conflict. He identified the problems and offered his solutions. *The Saturday Review* called it "one of the most important books ever written by an American businessman." For Johnson, the years of struggling to be heard were finally being rewarded.

Of all of the concepts embodied in the Credo, none became more visible to the general public than the series of handsome, modern plants that JOHNSON & JOHNSON began building in the mid-1930s. Later, of course, modern manufacturing centers became commonplace, but at that time most of American industry was still behind the walls of unappealing and drab-looking factories, many of them obsolete and some unsafe.

In 1934 it was decided to build a new plant for the Company's latest affiliate, Personal Products. Johnson surprised everyone by calling in the widely heralded architectural firm of Shreve, Lamb and Harmon that had only recently completed work on the dramatic new 102-story Empire State Building. Having designed the world's tallest skyscraper, the architects were somewhat nonplussed to find that what Johnson had in mind was a one-story building. It had to be expandable in all four directions, and the new plant — he detested calling them factories — was to

utilize all of the latest building materials, such as aluminum and plastics. Johnson had the initial design modified by his own construction staff, and then added his own ideas. Over the next several years the Company began building a series of modern plants in Central New Jersey, and the JOHNSON & JOHNSON tradition for building unusually attractive facilities became firmly established.

The facades of the buildings were all of a different design; the one most talked about was done in marble. But all of the buildings had clean lines and were superbly functional. Of paramount importance, they had to be located on large, attractively landscaped sites that often exceeded several hundred acres. Vast expanses of tinted glass were used so that workers could look out and enjoy the pastoral setting. Manufacturing areas were bright and airy and often air-conditioned. The walls were done in pastel colors, as were the specially designed covers that shielded the moving parts of all production machinery. These kept oily bearings from soiling the white nurse-type uniforms that had become a tradition with women employees since the Company's earliest days. There were strict rules on housekeeping, and when they were violated, heads rolled.

The plush lobbies and reception areas resembled movie sets, some with floor-to-ceiling windows, velvet drapes and recessed lighting. Employees were encouraged to use the lobby entrances and this promoted the feeling that it was their plant.

When asked why he went to such great expense to build plants of this quality, Johnson had a ready answer. In the long run, he said, they were less expensive. His employees took pride in their workplace, morale was high, and this assured greater output and higher quality products. What's more, he added, the plants were an asset to the community, and all of this might have been lost if the Company had lower standards. Johnson summed it up best at a ceremony opening one of the new plants, when he said: "We build not only structures such as this in which men and women will work, but also the pattern of society in which they will work. We are building not only frameworks of stone and steel, but frameworks of ideas and ideals."

As the business grew, so did JOHNSON & JOHNSON's reputation for being a skilled marketer of consumer products, and an innovator of creative advertising that also happened to sell products. In the late 1940s two unusual advertising campaigns added considerably to this reputation; both came from Young & Rubicam, a young ad agency rapidly gaining prominence and closely identified with JOHNSON & JOHNSON's continued success.

The advertising of MODESS brand sanitary napkins made by Personal Products had been less than successful. Because of his interest in the product, Robert Johnson often attended the advertising strategy meetings. On this particular day Johnson suggested that the next campaign be pegged to high fashion, a subject of known interest to many women. He cautioned, however, that if it were to be successful the designer clothes, the models, the settings and the photographers all would have to be far different than anything ever seen in magazine advertising.

Taking Johnson at his word, the product director and the agency account executives set out to do something radically different with a high fashion theme. Many of

the great couturieres — Valentina, Falkenstein, Hattie Carnegie, Balenciaga, Jacques Fath, Christian Dior — were engaged to design gowns to be used exclusively for the MODESS ads. Famous fashion models, including Dorian Leigh and Susie Parker, were photographed by such notables as Ruzzie Green, Cecil Beaton and Valentino Sarra. The exotic settings ranged from Park Avenue penthouses and European palaces to Venetian canals, art museums of the world, and the snowcapped mountains of Switzerland.

The "MODESS… *because*" campaign was an immediate success and was later chosen as one of the hundred all-time great advertisements. Sales of MODESS soared. But of all of its clever aspects, the simple two words of the copy, "MODESS… *because*" were the most ingenious. Actually that, too, was Johnson's suggestion, according to a marketing executive present the day it was suggested. "When it came to the question of copy," he recalled, "we knew from past experience that women resisted reading about a sanitary napkin, no matter how well written. We were discussing this problem with General Johnson, and he said: "Think in terms of as few words as possible, perhaps only ten

Modess …. *because*

words, maybe only five words, maybe only one word, just 'MODESS,' maybe 'MODESS… *because*.'" The brilliance of the "MODESS…*because*" copy was that it enabled each woman who read it to fill in her own reasons for wanting to buy the product.

Gladys Rockmore Davis was a noted American artist who mostly painted children. Her works were in the permanent collections at the Metropolitan Museum of Art and widely exhibited elsewhere. In 1948 JOHNSON & JOHNSON commissioned her to do a series of original paintings of children for use in an advertising campaign for first aid products. Madison Avenue was exuberant, claiming that it was the first time that the work of a noted artist was being wedded to advertising. The first of the series appeared in full page and full color advertisements in *Life* magazine and the *Saturday Evening Post* in the spring of 1949 and touched off a clamorous demand for reprints. Johnson & Johnson received thousands of requests and soon the Gladys Rockmore Davis advertisements were hanging in nurseries, kitchens and doctors' offices all across the country. The series ran for two years and included fifteen Gladys Rockmore Davis paintings.

"*Mommy always says you're safe when you use Johnson & Johnson*"

New exclusive formula: Now Red Cross* Adhesive Tape gives better sticking qualities and greater freedom from skin irritations.

Red Cross* Cotton comes to you sterile. This long-fibered cotton is the whitest, softest, most absorbent surgical cotton available.

Sealed in individual envelopes, Red Cross* Sterile Gauze Pads are soft, absorbent, absolutely sterile. Ideal for First Aid and Baby Care.

Fine mesh, pliable gauze with clean-cut edges, Red Cross* Gauze Bandages ravel less, stay neater. Famous for sterility and quality.

Individually wrapped and sterile, BAND-AID Adhesive Bandages are convenient protection for small cuts, blisters, and abrasions.

*No connection whatever with American National Red Cross.

The most trusted name in surgical dressings… Johnson & Johnson

PROFESSIONAL SKILLS
protect your health

PROFESSIONAL SKILL
at your Pharmacy

COTTON BALLS

BAND-AID

PRO

at

Johnson & Johnson

The most trusted name in surgical dressings

NO CONNECTION WHATEVER WITH AMERICAN NATIONAL RED CROSS.

S-977

Since its earliest days JOHNSON & JOHNSON had established a close working relationship with hospitals. Long before new hospitals opened their doors, Company representatives and the medical staff were conferring on ways to improve the care and safety of patients. These discussions often centered on the centuries-old question of controlling the twin hazards of infection and cross-contamination, areas in which JOHNSON & JOHNSON had become very knowledgeable. While the practice of surgery had made gigantic strides, the danger of infection was nearly as grave as when Lister sprayed his operating room with carbolic acid to fend off what he termed "unseen assassins."

Following World War II, the introduction of the first of the antibiotic "miracle" drugs captured the attention of the medical world. Behind the scenes, however, were numerous other less dramatic advances, among them the introduction of disposable products for use in hospitals. Many hospitals were still laundering, inspecting, folding, sorting, mending, wrapping and sterilizing linens, and even their surgical dressings. The introduction of non-woven textiles by Chicopee after a decade of research led to a new generation of hospital disposable products.

With the advent of disposables came new ways to enhance asepsis in hospitals; many of these concepts resulted from research by JOHNSON & JOHNSON. Imparting this information to hospitals and medical professionals required broad-scale educational programs, a role which the Company eagerly undertook, as it had so many times in the past.

As medical science advanced, the management of hospitals became more complicated. At the time there was no formal training for hospital administrators, a void that puzzled Robert Johnson. He had devoted many years to studying the role of hospital management, and had often lamented the lack of training for this role. In 1943 Johnson made a grant to Northwestern University to start the nation's first formal training program for hospital administrators, and the modern era of hospital management was under way.

Some of Johnson's other concepts on hospital organization were equally visionary. In 1931 he had prepared guidelines for hospitals which suggested that medical staffs should be organized according to specialties, such as surgery, obstetrics, radiology and pediatrics. At the time only a few

hospitals were organized along these lines, but in time it would become common practice.

Johnson's interest in medicine was wide ranging, and physicians rewarded his contributions with many honors. There were two he especially cherished: he was the first layman to receive an honorary fellowship from the American College of Surgeons, and the first American to become a member of the Court of Patrons of the Royal College of Surgeons in England.

Johnson was a hospital patient numerous times, and always with memorable results. Once he was required to get four shots of penicillin a day, and repeatedly the nurses would ask: "And where did we get the shot last time?" Annoyed, he sent out for an indelible pencil. Then, after each shot was administered, he drew a circle around the spot and noted the date. Soon his skin was covered with his notations, but it did put an end to the questions. On another hospital stay he decided to help reorganize the nurses' training program, which he accomplished in two weeks. Before leaving he also pledged to build a new medical library for the teaching institution. It had been a costly but gratifying stay.

In 1954 JOHNSON & JOHNSON sales were approaching $245 million, earnings were nearly $13 million, and the Company joined a select group of corporations that had paid cash dividends for fifty consecutive years. Increased emphasis was now being placed on product diversification as a way of sustaining continued growth. While many new products were developed from within, others came from new acquisitions. The temptation to buy new companies, however, was dampened by Johnson's oft-repeated admonition: "Never acquire a business that you don't know how to manage." Yet he went to great lengths to encourage his product managers to make bold decisions. "Failure is our most important product," he told them repeatedly, but the fact was the ranks of those who failed with new products were noticeably thinner than those who had succeeded.

Efforts to diversify resulted in some strange additions to the traditional JOHNSON & JOHNSON product lines—including hair brushes, a disposable toilet mop, automobile seat cover fabrics, iron-on tapes to mend clothing, and milk filters for the dairy industry.

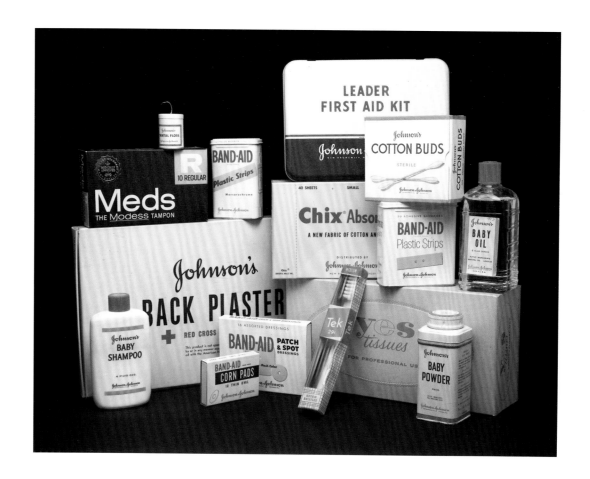

CONSUMER PRODUCTS

FIRST AID
BAND-AID Plastic Strips
BAND-AID Spots and Patches
RED CROSS Bandages
RED CROSS Cotton Balls
RED CROSS Sterile Gauze Pads
First Aid Kits

PERSONAL
BAND-AID Corn Pads
COETS Cotton Squares
FLEX-ACTION Hair Brushes
HUGHES Hair Brushes
JOHNSON'S Back Plasters
JOHNSON Dental Floss
MEDS Tampons
MODESS Sanitary Napkins and Belts
TEK Tooth Brushes
YES Facial Tissues

BABY
CHIX Crib Sheets
CHIX Diaper Liners
CHIX Gauze Diapers
CHUX Disposable Diapers
JOHNSON'S Baby Lotion
JOHNSON'S Baby Oil
JOHNSON'S Baby Powder
JOHNSON'S Baby Shampoo
JOHNSON'S Cotton Buds
REDI-FOL Diapers
SWANSOFT Crib Sheets
SWANSOFT Gauze Diapers

HOUSEHOLD
BONDEX Hot Iron Tape
CHICOPEE Fiberglas Screening
JONNY MOP Disposable Toilet Mop
LUMITE Saran Screening
MASSLINN Napkins and Towels
TEXCEL Cellophane Tape

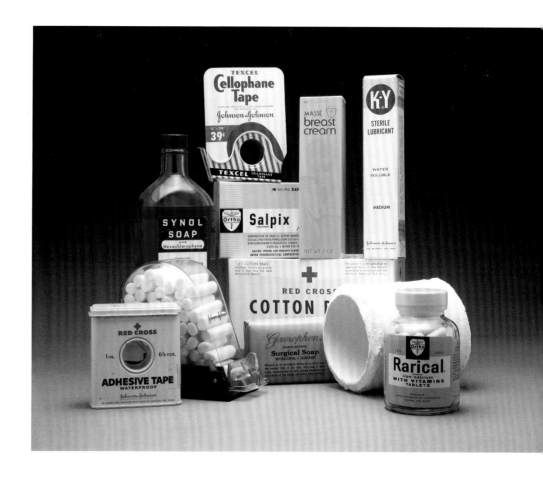

COMMERCIAL PRODUCTS

INDUSTRIAL AND AUTOMOTIVE
Bondex Heat Sealing Tape
Chicopee Seat Cover Fiber
Chixon Seat Cover Fabrics
Chix-Spun Upholstery Fabrics
Lumite Seat Cover Fabrics
Lumite Automotive Body Cloth
Masslinn Non-Woven Fabrics
Permacel Abrasives
Permacel Automotive Tapes
Permacel Industrial Tapes
Permacel Steel Wool
Permacel Tape Dispensers
Rapid-Flo Milk Filter Disks
Molded Plastic Products

TEXTILE
Bouffanette Nylon Horsehair
Chix Bookbinding Supers
Chix Cheesecloth
Chix Interlinings
Chix Plant Bed Covers
Flairform Shape Liner
Buckram
Crinoline
Print Cloth
Rayon and Sunthetic Fabrics
Tobacco Cloth

PROFESSIONAL PRODUCTS

MEDICAL AND SURGICAL
Atraloc Surgical Needles
Bio-Sorb Dusting Powder
Ethicon Surgical Sutures
Gamophen Surgical Soap
Johnson's Face Masks and Caps
K-Y Lubricating Jelly
Nu-Wrap Bandage Rolls
Ray-Tec X-Rayable Sponges
Red Cross Adhesive Tape
Red Cross Cotton
Specialist Plaster of Paris Bandages
Synol Liquid Soap
Tri-Pad Disposable Underpads
Zoroc Bandages

DENTAL
Dentoform Absorbent Cotton
Masslinn Professional Towels
Dental Cotton Rolls
Exodontia Sponges
Throat Packs

THERAPEUTIC AND DIAGNOSTIC
Aci-Jel Therapeutic Jelly
Gentersal Cream
Massé Cream
Nidoxital Capsules
Ortho Blood Diagnostic Sera
Rarical Iron and Calcium Tablets
Salpix Contrast Medium
Triple Sulfa Cream

The invention of the BAND-AID Brand Adhesive Bandage in 1920 set the stage for one of the most colorful success stories in the history of consumer marketing. The original product was an unwieldly eighteen inches long, and the user had to snip off pieces of the bandage to a desired size as needed. Early sales were dismal: there was no hint that someday the BAND-AID Adhesive Bandage would become one of the most popular consumer products of all time.

Later, when machinery was developed to make individual bandages, the market perked up and attracted a slew of competing brands led by Bauer & Black, a company founded by a former JOHNSON & JOHNSON sales manager. This was to become a classic marketing war that was waged for decades. In the 1930s, advertising focused on which product had the better adhesive. In one ad JOHNSON & JOHNSON claimed it had "A slicker, quicker sticker," and in another that the BAND-AID product "sticks like a day coach window." In 1943 both companies added the new wonder drug sulphathiazole to the adhesive bandage pad, and a new phase of the competition began. Then JOHNSON &

Johnson tried to capitalize on its valuable trademark with this advertising slogan:

"All Sparklers
Aren't Diamonds
All Adhesive Bandages
Aren't BAND-AID."

In 1951 when the two companies introduced plastic adhesive bandages, sales soared. The BAND-AID Brand introduced "Super-Stick," and Bauer & Black later countered with the first colored bandages for children, the "Curad Battle Ribbon," JOHNSON & JOHNSON came back with colored adhesive bandages called BAND-AID Stars 'n Stripes, and the fad raged on until youngsters began using the colored bandages when they didn't have cuts, and parents put their foot down. In time the bottom dropped out of the novelty market, but not before colored adhesive bandages triggered another fad, colored casting materials made of plaster of Paris. They were introduced by JOHNSON & JOHNSON with great fanfare, and were especially popular with children confined to hospitals. But colored casts met an early demise when the pure food dyes turned bed linens into a symphony of colors and hospital laundries into bedlam.

The introduction of BAND-AID Sheer Strips in 1958 propelled the once simple BAND-AID

Bandage into the world of high technology. Literally hundreds of improvements were being made to the product, and with each one JOHNSON & JOHNSON strengthened its market leadership. Every time the "ultimate" BAND-AID Brand Adhesive Bandage was developed, someone in the Company would come up with a new idea. Adhesive bandages have now been developed in all shapes and sizes from extra large to those that fit on fingertips. There have been versions with vents and mesh, some medicated and others flexible. The latest is BAND-AID Clear Strips, which blend so well with various skin tones that being inconspicuous is one of their major features. The product may be inconspicuous, but its success is quite evident, and adds another chapter to the remarkable story of the BAND-AID Adhesive Bandage.

In the decade following 1945, the JOHNSON & JOHNSON Family of Companies embarked upon an extensive program of plant and office expansion. New facilities were added in California, Georgia, Illinois, New Jersey and Texas. Of all the new additions, none was more striking than the new Ethicon, Inc. headquarters at Bridgewater, New Jersey. The long, gleaming white structure, with its distinctive blue-tinted glass and attractive landscaping, became the Company's showcase facility in New Jersey.

In 1956 the handsome new Ortho Pharmaceutical (Canada) Ltd. plant was opened in Toronto, setting the tone for many of the JOHNSON & JOHNSON international facilities that would soon be built. That same year affiliate companies were established in Germany, Venezuela and the Philippines. Introducing JOHNSON & JOHNSON products to a new international market usually began with representation by a sales agent. When consumer or medical demand

increased to the point of supporting an affiliate company, it was formed and usually managed by nationals of that country. All began as relatively small operations, but most of them grew rapidly. By now the Company had established some twenty-five international affiliates. JOHNSON & JOHNSON's long policy of having a strong cash position enabled plant expansion to continue despite dips in the world economy.

Ethicon, Inc.

Ortho Pharmaceutical, Canada

Henry S. McNeil; his father, Robert L. McNeil; and architect

JOHNSON & JOHNSON'S decision to enter the pharmaceutical field did not come easily. Some members of top management, including General Johnson himself, stubbornly resisted moving away from the Company's traditional product lines into the more risky and uncertain area of prescription medicines. One strong supporter of the move was George F. Smith, President of the Company, who had taken a leadership role in the industry as the first president of the Washington-based Pharmaceutical Manufacturers Association in 1958. Smith was concerned about the Company's long-term growth potential as well as its "BAND-AID" and "baby powder" image. He contended that JOHNSON & JOHNSON was more than that, and indeed it was, having developed a highly diverse family of companies and an increasingly sophisticated research program that included one of the world's leading scientists in the field of hematology, Dr. Philip Levine, director of the Ortho Research Foundation. It was Dr. Levine's work that led to the discovery of the Rh blood factor, which in turn enabled his colleagues some years later to develop a vaccine that was a preventative for Rh hemolytic disease of the newborn.

After finally resolving to enter the pharmaceutical field, the Company's early attempts to develop a business from within gained little headway. It was then that a search began for a highly reputable mid-size company to acquire. Early in 1959 McNeil Laboratories, Inc., of Philadelphia became an affiliate of JOHNSON & JOHNSON. It was a family-owned business that traced its origins to a drugstore opened in the mill district of Philadelphia in 1879. The business prospered, and in 1900 a manufacturing laboratory for pharmaceuticals was added in an upstairs room. This successful venture grew to become McNeil Laboratories, with a strong reputation for product integrity and a close relationship with the medical community. McNeil specialized in sedation and muscle-relaxant drugs, and later introduced TYLENOL. That same year Cilag Chemie, a small Swiss pharmaceutical firm, was acquired by JOHNSON & JOHNSON.

Around this same time word had reached the Company of the brilliant pharmacologi-

cal research being done by a young Belgian physician, Dr. Paul Janssen. Borrowing $1,000 from his physician father in 1953, Dr. Janssen had opened a laboratory in the town of Beerse and, with two untrained assistants, had gone to work. In the next several years he discovered two original compounds that became successful pharmaceutical products. In 1961 Janssen Pharmaceutica, still small but highly productive in research, joined the JOHNSON & JOHNSON Family of Companies. Over time, Dr. Janssen became one of the most prolific and highly regarded pharmacological researchers in the world.

Dr. Paul A. J. Janssen

Dr. Philip Levine

Robert W. Johnson, Jr.

JOHNSON & JOHNSON'S rapid growth led to an important change in the management structure in 1954, when the Executive Committee of the Board of Directors was formed. The size of the Board—twenty-three members—had become unwieldy, so Robert Johnson decided to form an Executive Committee of seven members to make key decisions. The formation of the Executive Committee set a pattern for the Company's future management organization at the top level.

The youngest member of the first Executive Committee was 34-year-old Robert Wood Johnson, Jr., the third generation of his family to enter the business. Known to all as Bobby, Johnson had spent four summers during his college years working in various production jobs in order to learn the business from the ground up, much the same as his father had. Bobby was personable and quickly made friends with the mill and factory workers, who were delighted to have a new Johnson protege to break in. When he joined the Company full-time, Johnson held a variety of jobs—in construction, personnel, and manufacturing— before selecting

merchandising and advertising as his career. He later became head of marketing at a time when new techniques in consumer research and test marketing were being used for the first time. There were new opportunities in advertising as well, since television was just making its debut. Johnson was a very creative marketing person with excellent instincts for building brand loyalty in consumer products. Sensing how competitive the market was becoming for JOHNSON & JOHNSON, he brought in a new breed of brand managers and gave them broad responsibilities as well as ample advertising and marketing budgets. The results were successful, but Bobby Johnson and his marketing

group continued to make bold and sometimes controversial decisions. The marketing group was headquartered in Johnson Hall, the handsome then-new Georgian Colonial home of the various product divisions. It was separated by a courtyard from the antiquated Kilmer House, home of the corporate hierarchy. At times the tiny courtyard seemed like an abyss and the journey across it interminable. Bobby Johnson made that journey frequently to present his marketing plans, and sometimes he would encounter stiff opposition. When the smoke of battle cleared, often the only two combatants still left in the arena were young Johnson and his father. Their frequent disagreements over marketing and advertising decisions were, many believed, an extension of differences that were rooted in the past. Both had an intense loyalty to the Company, and for years this remained the ground for compromise. But later, in one of the Company's sadder moments, Bobby Johnson was to resign after four years as President of JOHNSON & JOHNSON, following a serious altercation with his father. They reconciled their differences shortly before the father's death several years later, and Bobby Johnson died two years after that.

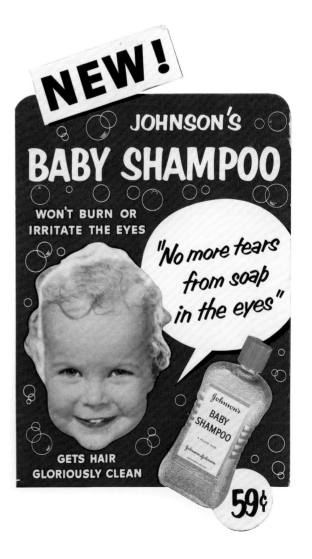

characterized JOHNSON & JOHNSON's print and radio advertising was now helping to shape the Company's public image on television. But with TV, it was important to select shows that epitomized wholesome family programming. The first major choice was "The Adventures of Robin Hood," a series of derring-do dramas revolving around the legendary hero of England's Sherwood Forest. Produced against the backdrop of the storied forest and other locales of the famous legend, the teleplays featured an array of characters—Little John, Friar Tuck, Maid Marian—and Robin Hood's

When commercial television burst upon the scene in the early 1950s, JOHNSON & JOHNSON was poised and ready to capitalize on the exciting new medium that had captivated all of America. At first many advertisers were wary of television, but JOHNSON & JOHNSON made an early decision to become one of TV's first major sponsors.

It was a good move, for in a short time television helped strengthen the Company's leadership position in baby and first aid products. The same good taste that

other cohorts as they contested the Sheriff of Nottingham in their quest to see that riches were shared.

The story is probably apocryphal, but General Johnson was traveling overseas when the 26-week series first aired. After returning and viewing the antics of Robin Hood on the television screen, Johnson supposedly called one of the Company's advertising executives and asked: "What is this business about stealing from the rich and giving to the poor?" Despite Robin Hood's indiscretions with the rich, JOHNSON & JOHNSON continued sponsoring the program for three years. Other early television successes that the Company sponsored included the "Donna Reed Show," "Cheyenne," and "Gunsmoke."

From 1970 to 1985 the Company's television advertising budget climbed from $10 million a year to well over $165 million, ranking it among the top ten network TV advertisers in the country. The commercials continued to enhance the Company's reputation for good taste in its advertising.

No other bandage sticks

BAND-AID Plastic
TRADE-MARK

AMAZING BOILING WATER TEST

1. To see how eager this new SUPER-STICK adhesive is to take hold, just touch the end of a BAND-AID Plastic Strip to an egg.

2. Without any pressure, this bandage sticks —and so firmly you can lift the egg (a dry egg, of course, at room temperature).

3. It stays on—even when you plunge the egg into boiling water.

Philip B. Hofmann

In the spring of 1963, Robert Johnson, at the age of seventy, decided to step down as Chairman and Chief Executive Officer. For fifty-three years his presence had exerted an enormous influence on JOHNSON & JOHNSON. He had served as President and Chairman for thirty-one of those years, and was determined to see to it that his departure was not disruptive to the Company. He had carefully selected and trained his successor, Philip B. Hofmann, whose career with the Company began in 1931 as a shipping clerk, a year after his graduation from college. Hofmann was the son of an Iowa druggist, and began his rise through the Company's ranks as a salesman. His aggressive and often flamboyant style impressed Johnson, and he had led the Company into two highly successful areas of business, family planning with Ortho and surgical sutures with Ethicon.

During his long career, Johnson had helped establish the Company's style of management and its culture, and many wondered how different JOHNSON & JOHNSON would be without him. The difference, as it turned out, was barely noticeable, which is precisely the way Johnson had planned it. His

Gustav O. Lienhard

management principles were solidly in place, and it had been his policy to develop a well trained and generously rewarded group of executives, all of whom had sizable stock holdings in the Company. They had been given all of the encouragement and incentive they needed to make the business successful, for in many respects they saw themselves as owner-managers of JOHNSON & JOHNSON.

Under Hofmann's leadership, the Company's sales during the next six years doubled from $500 million to over a billion. The goal of one billion was reached in 1970 in tribute to the impending retirement of Gustav O. Lienhard, President and Chairman of the Executive Committee. Lienhard's shrewd financial management had greatly influenced the Company's progress for decades. Johnson used to jokingly refer to him as "the penurious Mr. Lienhard," but there was no better guardian of the corporate treasury and his efforts guaranteed that the Company would have the financial resources necessary for future growth.

Though he was officially retired, Johnson could not bring himself to be completely out of the mainstream of managing the business. He remained on the Board, with the title of Chairman of the Finance Committee, and in that capacity had his say about the Company's fiscal policies. Johnson was also heard from frequently on matters related to marketing and advertising, since he had never cured himself of the habit of patrolling drugstores and supermarkets wherever he went. On these store visits he critically assessed how JOHNSON & JOHNSON products were faring against the competition, and then would send back bristling notes to the marketing department listing his suggestions. Johnson had a keen eye for packaging and advertising, and many of his points were valid and resulted in changes. Other times his suggestions were quietly and very diplomatically set aside.

While no longer a part of the day-to-day operations, Johnson never stopped worrying about the Company he was leaving behind. On that subject he once commented: "I am leaving a business, not money, and it is of great importance to me to maintain the integrity and personality of that business." In that sense, Johnson never left the Company.

The Board of Directors in 1963 represented a bridge between the past, the present, and the next generation of management of JOHNSON & JOHNSON. Robert Wood Johnson had just stepped down as Chairman of the Board, and was succeeded by Philip B. Hofmann, with Gustav O. Lienhard serving as President and Chairman of the Executive Committee. Richard B. Sellars would be the next to become Chairman a decade later. The twenty-three members of the Board collectively represented 581 years of service to JOHNSON & JOHNSON, an average of about twenty-five years each.

FRONT ROW,
Left to Right
Robert W. Johnson, Jr.
Robert J. Dixson
Richard B. Sellars
Wayne J. Holman, Jr.
Philip B. Hofmann
General Robert W. Johnson
Claude V. Swank
Gustav O. Lienhard
Harry C. McKenzie

BACK ROW,
Left to Right
George W. Achenbach
John J. Smith
Henry S. McNeil
L. Russell Feakes
Andrew A. Rohlfing
Richard V. Mulligan
Thomas O. Boucher
Vincent J. Robinson
Dr. William H. Lycan
Robert L. McNeil
Foster B. Whitlock
J. Seward Johnson
August J. Bee
John J. Gibson

ARGENTINA
  Buenos Aires, Pilar

AUSTRALIA
  Botany, Melbourne,
  Rosebery, Sydney

AUSTRIA • Vienna

COLOMBIA • Barranquilla

BELGIUM • Beerse, Turnhout

ECUADOR • Guayaquil

GERMANY • Alsbach,
  Düsseldorf, Hamburg

BRAZIL
  São José dos Campos,
  São Paulo

ENGLAND • Earby, Gargrave,
  High Wycombe, London,
  Portsmouth, Slough

HOLLAND
  Amersfoort, Cuyk, Tilburg

IRELAND • Tallagh

CANADA • Montreal,
  Peterborough, Port Credit,
  Toronto

FRANCE • Paris

INDIA • Bombay, Mulund

ITALY • Milan

orld-Wide Operations

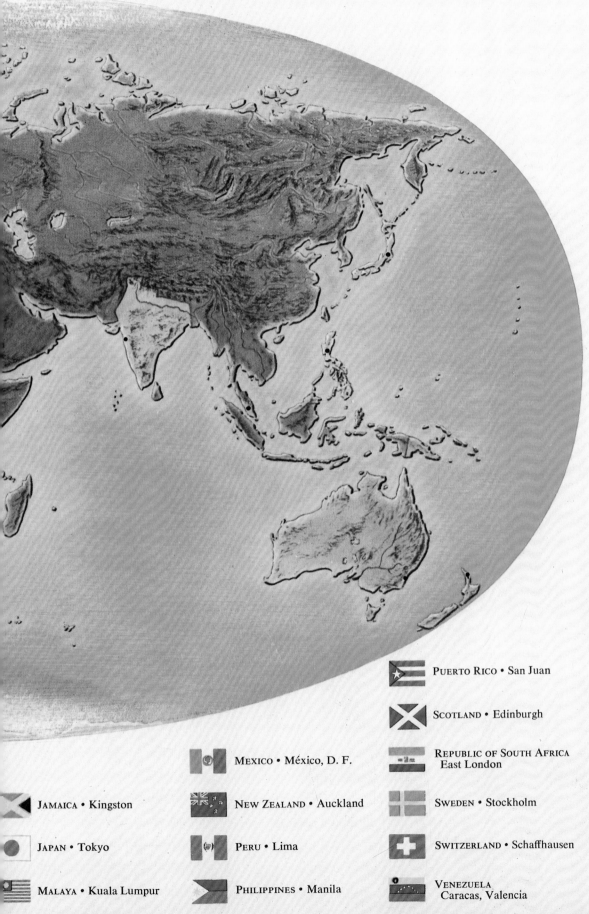

In the 1964 Annual Report to Stockholders, the Company proudly recognized its thirty years of international operations. That year alone, new plant or office facilities were begun in seven countries. International sales were approaching $120 million, and earnings were just under $7 million. The international building program continued at a then rapid pace, with plant and equipment expenditures rising to nearly $11 million in 1965.

JAMAICA • Kingston

JAPAN • Tokyo

MALAYA • Kuala Lumpur

MEXICO • México, D. F.

NEW ZEALAND • Auckland

PERU • Lima

PHILIPPINES • Manila

PUERTO RICO • San Juan

SCOTLAND • Edinburgh

REPUBLIC OF SOUTH AFRICA
East London

SWEDEN • Stockholm

SWITZERLAND • Schaffhausen

VENEZUELA
Caracas, Valencia

Robert W. Johnson

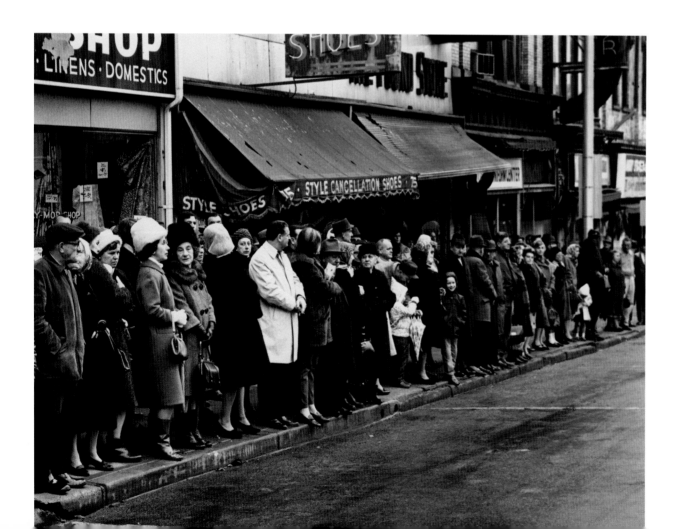

On January 30, 1968, Robert Wood Johnson died at Roosevelt Hospital in New York, at the age of seventy-four. In the days that followed, many people reflected on his life and accomplishments, but their attempts to define Johnson after his death proved just as difficult as when he was alive. He had been a man of many parts, and was dynamic, restless, outspoken and unconventional in all of them.

In his final days in the hospital he astonished the medical staff by having the strength and determination to sketch out a design he had in mind for a new type of hospital bed. Johnson explained that he had always found hospital beds uncomfortable, and had wanted to improve them. He was also unconventional in other ways. A few years earlier he was spending an evening at home with his wife, Evelyne, when she sensed that the book he was reading was making him increasingly irritated. Suddenly, he asked her if she would go for a drive with him. They drove silently for several miles, to a bridge that crossed a swift-flowing brook. He stopped the car on the bridge and threw the book into the water. Then, satisfied that the book had been properly dealt with, he got in the car and drove home.

Though he was one of the nation's wealthiest industrialists, Johnson had always been considered a friend by the working classes. On their behalf he had fought for higher wages and lower hours, clean and modern plants, and a heightened sense of human dignity for all workers. As it turned out, he was a friend to many. When his will was made known it was learned that he had left $1.2 billion, the bulk of his estate, to the Robert Wood Johnson Foundation to improve health care in the nation. All of a sudden, the tiny foundation —then headquartered in a modest

Early Robert Wood Johnson Foundation Office

home in New Brunswick — became the second largest in the nation, and the primary one devoted to improving health care.

Because of his magnanimous gift to society, Johnson would be remembered as a humanitarian; that tended to obscure his other roles as a business leader, public servant, political figure, author, and conservationist. It also overshadowed the expertise he brought to hospital management, mass transportation, ocean racing, piloting a plane, and various other pursuits as well. When Johnson was praised before the House of Representatives, its members chose to refer to him as "a patriot whose love for America was as deep as his love for people."

Your touch tells him everything.
That's why we make our baby powder so pure and soft and soothing.
It feels like love.

Johnson's baby powder

Johnson & Johnson

JOHNSON's Baby Powder advertising has always been an important hallmark of the Company, and over the years it has generated enormous good will. It has also helped to develop JOHNSON's Baby Powder into the most widely used baby product in the world.

In the mid-1960s, baby powder advertising took on even greater importance as it began to focus on the intensely important feelings generated between a mother and her newborn child. The more this relationship was understood, the more obvious it became that the most important function of baby toiletries was the facilitation of a mother's need to physically demonstrate love to her child. The whole process of changing diapers and bathing a child was enhanced by powders, oils, and lotions, and encouraged the mother to spend more time touching and caressing her baby.

More important, as this relationship was studied deeply, it became evident that this physical relationship had profound effects on the health and well-being of the child and, for that matter, on the mother as well.

JOHNSON & JOHNSON sponsored the first conference on this subject, bringing together pediatricians, psychiatrists, psychologists and other professionals, to explore the mother-child relationship more fully. The Company has continued to support research into the process now commonly called "nurturing," one recognized by most medical experts as being profoundly important to the healthy development of a child.

This professional understanding was truly catalyzed by the scientific work initiated by JOHNSON & JOHNSON a generation ago. The advertising that arose out of this understanding was called "The World of Feeling," and to this day this basic understanding of the importance of "touch" to both mother and baby is fundamental to the continuing success of baby toiletries and to the image of the corporation in every country in the world.

One of JOHNSON & JOHNSON's great strengths has always been its ability to carefully prepare its management people for the next level of responsibility, and then orchestrate a smooth transition. The continuity of management at the upper echelons has always been given careful thought, as though the top positions were some sort of sacred trust; there are those who will argue that it is. When Hofmann became Chairman, Richard B. Sellars was named President and Chairman of the Executive Committee. Then in April of 1973, Sellars, who began his career with the Company thirty-five years earlier as a salesman, became Chairman of the Board and Chief Executive Officer. Foster B. Whitlock, who had also started with JOHNSON & JOHNSON as a salesman thirty-five years earlier, was elected Vice Chairman of the Board, and James E. Burke became President and Chairman of the Executive Committee. Burke, who had been with the Company twenty years, had come up through the ranks in marketing.

Despite difficult problems posed by inflation, an economic recession and energy shortages, Sellars and his management team were able to maintain the Company's historic growth

rates. Between 1973 and 1976 worldwide sales increased by almost $1 billion, and earnings were up an average of over fourteen percent annually. Several new affiliated companies were formed, and Sellars placed great emphasis on drawing together the worldwide managements of JOHNSON & JOHNSON into a more cohesive group without threatening the autonomy they enjoyed as decentralized units. In 1975 the subject of business ethics and practices began receiving wide attention at all United States-based companies, when there were disclosures of illegal payments overseas. These problems prompted Sellars, who was one of the Company's staunchest supporters of the JOHNSON & JOHNSON Credo philosophy, to call for a rededication to the principles embodied in the document. Just prior to that, Burke had suggested to Sellars that there be a review of the way the Company management around the world viewed the Credo that Robert Johnson had written thirty years earlier. Burke said he suspected that many managers were paying only lip service to it, even though it hung on the walls of their offices. A "Credo Challenge" meeting was

called, and after two days of debate, the overwhelming majority of managers supported retaining the Credo philosophy, but urged some word changes to bring the document more in keeping with the times. By giving management the opportunity, through discussion and confrontation, to "buy into" the Credo, its philosophy became their philosophy as well, and not one foisted upon them by a previous generation. The dynamics of that meeting were

Richard B. Sellars and James E. Burke

so important that over the next three years a series of "Credo Challenge" meetings were held and they included the managing directors of every JOHNSON & JOHNSON company. The results were the same as those of the first meeting: the Credo philosophy was reaffirmed, and some word changes were recommended. In 1979 the revised Credo was reissued at a worldwide management meeting dedicated to the Credo. Its importance as an integral part of the JOHNSON & JOHNSON culture was reaffirmed, and this time it was a set of principles that all of the current management endorsed.

For several years a debate was carried on within JOHNSON & JOHNSON's management over the best location for a new corporate headquarters. In the years following World War II New Brunswick, like many other mid-size American cities, was suffering serious economic ills. Retail business felt the impact of new shopping malls and the city began to take on a shabby appearance. Many felt that by remaining in New Brunswick, where it had been since its founding in 1886, JOHNSON & JOHNSON would be at a disadvantage and be burdened with the city's many problems. There were many

better sites, they argued, in the rural areas of Central New Jersey. Sellars felt that if the Company left New Brunswick, all hope for revitalizing the city would be lost. Besides, he pointed out, one of the Credo tenets was responsibility to the community. As Chairman, he prevailed upon the Board to support his decision to have the Company remain in the city and build its new world headquarters there. Plans were formulated, and in the spring of 1978 the announcement of this decision gave New Brunswick a big psychological boost that got the rebuilding program off to a flying start and served as a catalyst for the revitalization of the city. Sellars had earlier stepped down as Chairman of the Company, but remained on the Board and also as Chairman of the Finance Committee. He then decided that he would personally take on the leadership of the revitalization effort.

Model of Johnson & Johnson headquarters planned for New Brusnwick, N.J.

Johnson & Johnson Is Expanding In Downtown New Brunswick, N.J.

NEW BRUNSWICK, N.J., April 6— Johnson & Johnson Inc. announced today that it would construct a new $50 million worldwide corporate headquarters in downtown New Brunswick.

The medical-supplies company, already the major taxpayer in this Middlesex County urban center, said it had spurned temptations to move its headquarters to suburban sites and that it was committed to the revitalization of this city of 40,0

Byrne, who attended th remony, said the "a significa New J

on a 12-acre tract at the "crossroads" of downtown New Brunswick.

With construction expected to start later this year, after the acquisition of all the necessary property has been completed, the project sho the m

It is doubtful that Dick Sellars realized the magnitude of the task he had volunteered for when he agreed to lead the revitalization of New Brunswick. Following his retirement from the Company he devoted the next ten years to the effort, which many thought was a dream, and some a fantasy. Sellars began by organizing New Brunswick Tomorrow as a policy planning coalition and persuading scores of business, academic, government, labor, community, and religious leaders to join him in the commitment. His closest associate in the effort was John J. Heldrich, a JOHNSON & JOHNSON executive who played a pivotal role and served as chairman of

New Brunswick Tomorrow from its inception in 1975.

Together they began the painfully slow rebuilding process. Both Sellars and Heldrich knew from the outset that the revitalization of an entire city would require more than just new buildings and an influx of retail businesses. It would mean finding new ways to strengthen the entire social fabric of the city, from the educational system to the cultural programs, and many other areas as well. But most important, they would have to find ways to bolster the sagging spirits of New Brunswick residents who had watched the city deteriorate and had begun to lose hope for its revival.

In the decade that followed, remarkable results were achieved. Improvements in downtown New Brunswick were dramatic. New construction totaling $300 million gave the business district a new face, replacing rows of dilapidated buildings with rows of new retail stores and offices. JOHNSON & JOHNSON's new corporate headquarters, occupying a twelve-acre site in the heart of the business area, was the first major addition. Architect I. M. Pei set out to design what he called "a building within a park, and a park within a

city," and he succeeded in creating a centerpiece for the downtown area. A wave of new construction followed, including a hotel, shopping malls, office buildings, a parking deck, and a $75 million expansion and renovation of the Robert Wood Johnson University Hospital. The second phase of construction, underway in 1986 and costing an additional $100 million, includes a four-building cultural center.

By 1986 the revitalization process had created some 4,000 new permanent jobs in a city with a population of about 50,000. Nearly $3 million annually in new tax revenue was helping to provide improved services for residents. Property values increased, and people began taking a new pride in the appearance of their homes and neighborhoods.

Once the momentum of physical-economic progress was established, New Brunswick Tomorrow focused its priorities on human services to translate revitalization into an improved quality of life. The programs it instituted include health care, family day care, education, jobs, and training. Through its financial support and the participation of some of its management specialists, JOHNSON & JOHNSON continues to play a leadership role.

In 1976, JOHNSON & JOHNSON was widely recognized as one of America's most successful companies, with a remarkable growth record. But it also faced a host of new challenges brought about by vast changes taking place in the nation's health care delivery system, and an explosion of new medical technologies. That year, James E. Burke, at age fifty-one, became JOHNSON & JOHNSON's fourth Chairman and Chief Executive Officer. David R. Clare was named President of JOHNSON & JOHNSON and Chairman of the Executive Committee. Clare was

fifty and had begun his career with the Company thirty years earlier as a manufacturing trainee.

A fundamental challenge confronting the new management was the need to keep JOHNSON & JOHNSON as competitive in the future as it had been in the past. The world was about to be caught up in a medical revolution driven by increasingly sophisticated consumers and burgeoning medical technologies that opened the way for new approaches to prevention,

James E. Burke

David R. Clare

early detection, and treatment of disease. Not keeping pace with these medical advances could mean stagnation for the business, though remaining in the forefront would require huge investments and a much higher level of risk.

In choosing the course of continued growth, the new management made a major commitment to research and development investments. The Corporate Office of Science and Technology, known as COSAT, was established in 1978. Its mission was to assist the affiliate companies in upgrading internal scientific competence, to discover

new resources applicable to the businesses JOHNSON & JOHNSON was already in, and to help identify new corporate opportunities in new science and technology.

In the coming years investments in research and development would increase four-fold, to well over $400 million a year, placing JOHNSON & JOHNSON eighteenth among all United States companies in research spending, and first in the health care field. JOHNSON & JOHNSON positioned itself with its major focus as a research-based company. Concurrent with this rededication to research, the Company accelerated its program of acquisitions, entering new areas of medicine for the first time. This helped strengthen JOHNSON & JOHNSON's position as the most diversified health care enterprise in the world, and the only company serving every one of the twenty-three medical specialties, from anesthesiology to urology.

Despite the uncertainties of the volatile health field and numerous unforeseen problems as well, JOHNSON & JOHNSON's growth in the decade following 1976 was dramatic. The number of international operating companies was nearly doubled, and worldwide sales increased from $2.5 billion in 1976 to close to $7 billion in 1986. Over half of all JOHNSON & JOHNSON's

total sales were in products that held the number one position in the marketplace.

Other changes were taking place within the Company as it expanded to include 160 companies in fifty-five countries; one change was in management style. Burke's way of approaching problems was to generate discussion. He not only tolerated contention but encouraged it. This led to renewed vitality within the organization. Clare, as Chairman of the Executive Committee, carried a large share of the responsibility for the management of the Company. He had a different style, though, taking more of an analytical approach. The two styles were vastly different, but they complemented each other very effectively and resulted in greater participation by more members of management in major decisions. These changes took place without altering the Company's traditional approach to management, which Burke often expressed in this way: "We believe the consistency of our overall performance as a corporation is due to our unique form of decentralized management, our adherence to the ethical principles embodied in our Credo, and our emphasis on managing the business for the long term."

The ability to leverage thousands of products, representing all of the medical specialties, to any of its 160 companies has long been one of JOHNSON & JOHNSON's important capabilities. Wherever health care needs and market demands are identified, there is the potential for the Company's presence. In the Company's 100th year an intriguing new marketing venture was being developed in the People's Republic of China, where Janssen Pharmaceutica was participating in the largest pharmaceutical joint venture ever undertaken in that nation. Several other business opportunities in China were also underway in 1986.

While the philosophy of decentralization still reigned supreme, the beginning of the Company's second century saw a growing synergy among the managements of all of the affiliate companies. This was enhanced by the Company's new organizational structure along the lines of business segments: consumer, pharmaceutical and diagnostics, and professional. The new structure permitted greater coordination of effort and purpose, as well as a forum for business decisions. This was accomplished without threatening the management autonomy that remained traditional throughout the Company's history.

CHICOPEE

CILAG

CODMAN & SHURTLEFF

CRITIKON

ETHICON

IOLAB

JANSSEN PHARMACEUTICA

JOHNSON & JOHNSON BABY PRODUCTS CO.

JOHNSON & JOHNSON CARDIOVASCULAR

JOHNSON & JOHNSON DENTAL PRODUCTS CO.

JOHNSON & JOHNSON PRODUCTS

MCNEIL CONSUMER PRODUCTS CO.

MCNEIL PHARMACEUTICAL

ORTHO DIAGNOSTIC SYSTEMS INC.

ORTHO PHARMACEUTICAL

PERSONAL PRODUCTS

SURGIKOS

VISTAKON

XANAR

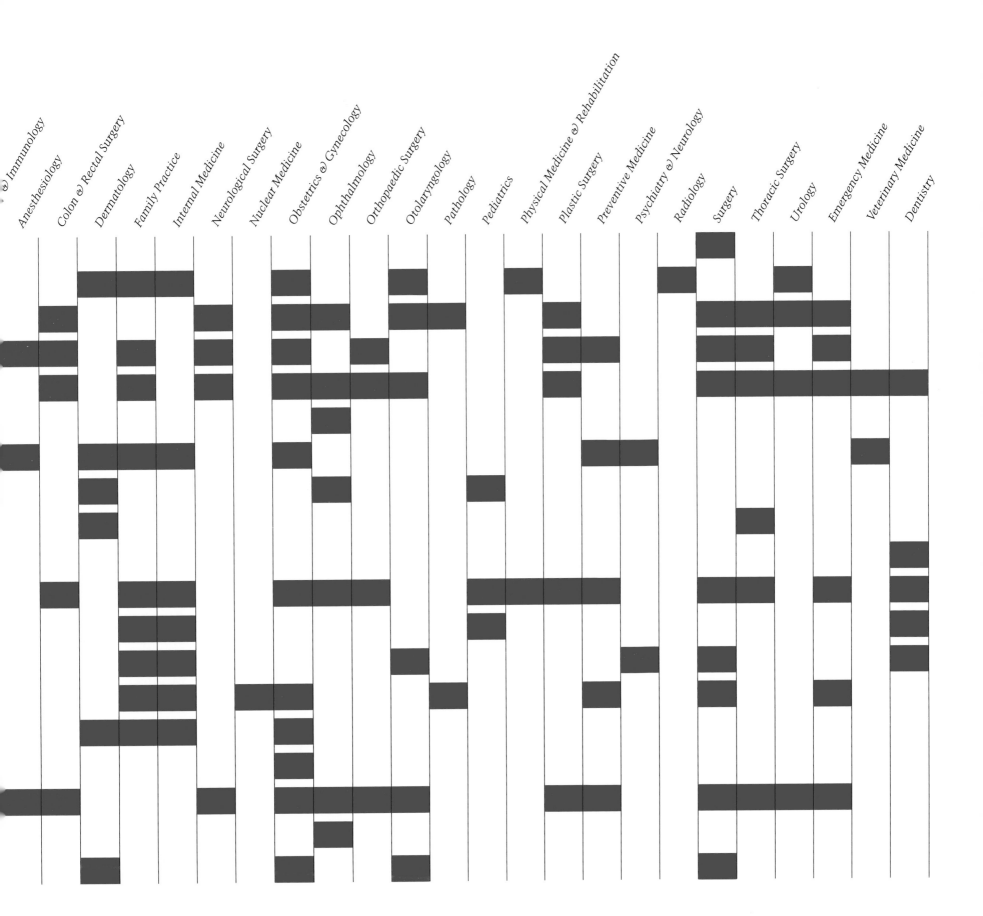

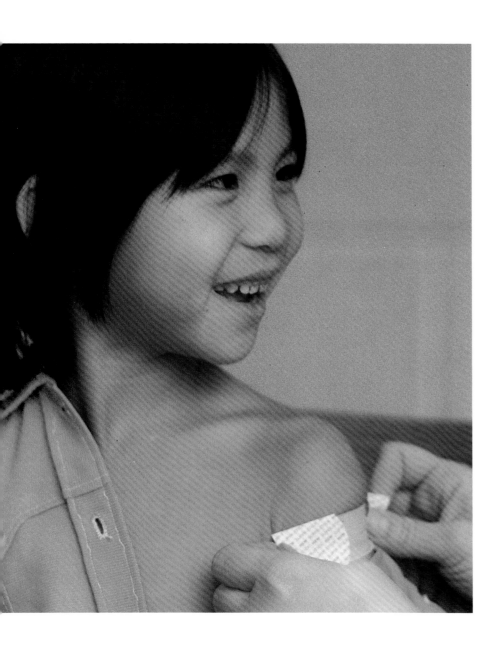

The consumer area is the largest of JOHNSON & JOHNSON's business segments. While represented by hundreds of different products, the four largest consumer franchises are in proprietary drugs, and baby, health care and female sanitary protection products. Few companies ever enjoyed such a strong presence in each of these major markets, or had as many products that have franchise leadership as well as longevity.

While the average new consumer product on the market in the health care field had a life span of about seven years,

Michael A. Sneed

more than one-third of JOHNSON & JOHNSON's consumer sales in 1986 came from products that had been on the market ten years or longer. Some, like the venerable JOHNSON's Baby Powder and BAND-AID Brand Adhesive Bandages, remained among the oldest consumer products still on the market.

New products also played a major role. Research and development investments in the consumer area resulted in important contributions to the Company's overall sales performance. New products introduced from 1980 to 1986 represented more than twenty-five percent of domestic consumer sales. Over the ten years beginning in 1976, JOHNSON & JOHNSON led all of its major competitors in the number of successful new products introduced in food stores in the United States in the health and beauty aids category. Franchise leadership was also an important factor. More than seventy percent of all of JOHNSON & JOHNSON's worldwide consumer sales in 1986 were from products in which the company held the leadership position in that market.

There emerged a strong trend toward the conversion of pharmaceutical and professional products to consumer product status. This was brought about by an increased willingness on the part of consumers to assume additional responsibility for monitoring their own health, such as with the use of home test kits. It also helped reduce costs. Since no company in the health care field was as broadly based in all three areas— pharmaceutical, professional and consumer—JOHNSON & JOHNSON was especially well positioned to capitalize on this trend.

Kathleen Martin

Jeffrey M. Nugent

Dr. Paul A. J. Janssen

Dennis N. Longstreet and Dr. Gideon Goldstein

From virtual obscurity twenty-five years earlier, pharmaceuticals had become the fastest growing segment of the Company's business by 1986, making JOHNSON & JOHNSON the seventh largest pharmaceutical company in the world.

The Company's pharmaceutical business, which included Janssen Pharmaceutica, McNeil Pharmaceutical, Ortho Pharmaceutical, and Cilag, had entries in fields representing twenty-nine percent of the world pharmaceutical market in 1986. Products that were in development at the time would increase it to sixty-two percent of the world

market. Janssen Pharmaceutica, under the guidance of its founder, Dr. Paul Janssen, had emerged as one of the most productive sources of new pharmaceutical products in the history of pharmacology. Janssen and his research team had developed sixty-six new pharmaceutical compounds over a span of thirty-three years. They included products in the fields of mycology, parasitology, psychiatry, gastroenterology, and blood circulation. To accomplish this, Janssen research teams synthesized some 68,000

David A. Cherry

Dr. James L. Bittle and Dr. Richard A. Houghten

original molecules in the years from 1953 to 1986. Three Janssen compounds were placed on the "essential drugs" list of the World Health Organization.

At an early date JOHNSON & JOHNSON placed strong emphasis on the promising field of biotechnology, both in its own laboratories and through agreements with small companies that began to emerge as leaders in the field. Internally, Dr. Gideon Goldstein's immunobiology program at Ortho—with original research in monoclonal antibodies and synthetic peptides—showed great promise. In 1986 Ortho brought to market the first monoclonal antibody approved for human therapeutic use in the world. An important research relationship was developed with the highly respected Scripps Research Institute in California, with exclusive rights to all products resulting from that research. Other areas in which JOHNSON & JOHNSON had begun focusing its pharmaceutical and diagnostics research included DNA probes, which allow for highly specific and very rapid testing to diagnose disease; the immunochemistry market, which represents a large segment with rapidly expanding new product opportunities; and infectious disease diagnostics, in which Ortho Diagnostic Systems had established itself as the market leader in herpes testing.

The Company perceived great opportunities in the pharmaceutical and diagnostic businesses, both in established areas and with new products. Also of interest was the prospect that some day selected pharmaceuticals and diagnostics might be converted to consumer products.

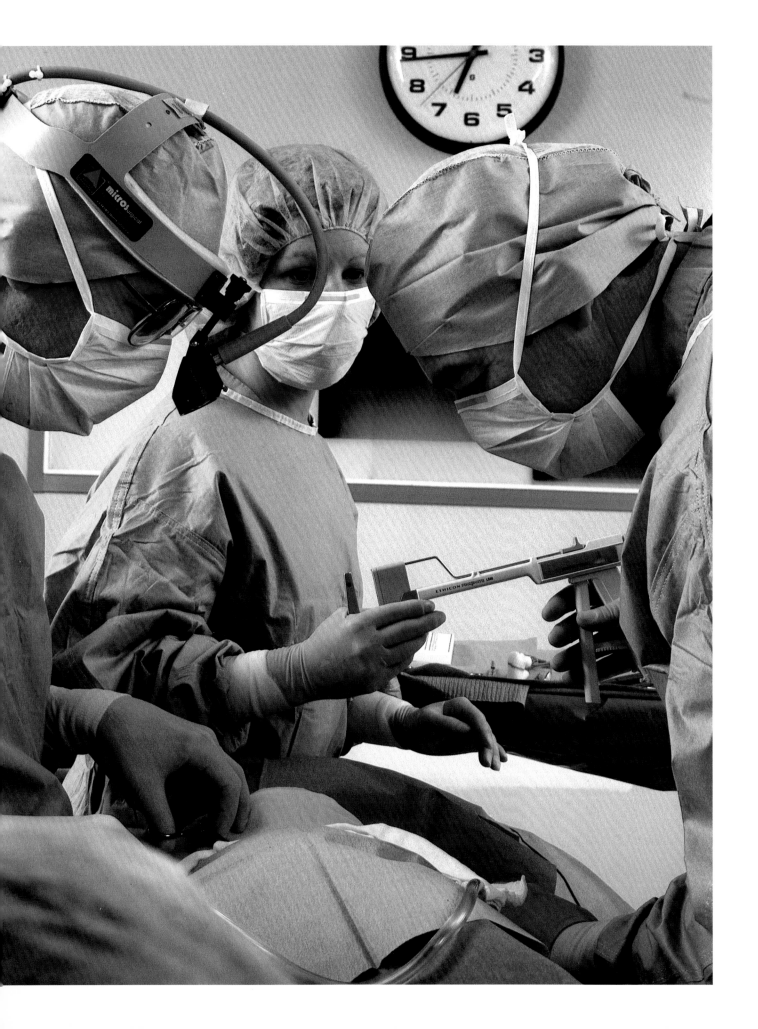

The history of professional products at JOHNSON & JOHNSON began with the Company's founding. Over the course of decades a sound relationship was established with physicians, nurses, and hospitals, centered primarily on product superiority and broad-based educational programs for medical professionals. Throughout its first 100 years JOHNSON & JOHNSON remained in the forefront of improved patient care.

Beginning in the 1970s, there was an explosion in health care costs, and this triggered rapid changes in the health system's reimbursement and delivery approaches. JOHNSON & JOHNSON foresaw these changes, including the need for more sophisticated technological and scientific approaches to retain its competitive edge in products. As a result, beginning in the late 1970s, the Company placed an unprecented emphasis on new product and improved product investment—both through research and the acquisition of companies and products. Over a period of fifteen years, research spending on professional products quintupled, and research and development expenditures as a percent of sales increased dramatically.

Between 1976 and 1985, thirty professional segment acquisitions were made, adding

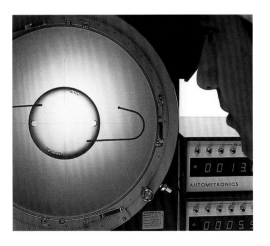

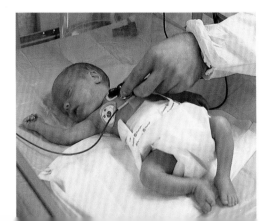

significantly to the Company's product range. These included the worldwide leaders in both intraocular lenses and blood pressure monitors, as well as one of the leading orthodontic companies.

One of the most significant changes in policy and strategy in the area of professional products was the formation of JOHNSON & JOHNSON Hospital Services. This new entity complemented the decentralized companies by enhancing overall distribution and marketing capabilities and providing a corporate interface with the emerging integrated health care delivery systems. The COACT On-Line Procurement System improved service and was designed to reduce costs and make it easier to do business with JOHNSON & JOHNSON's professional companies.

The professional sector continued to focus on major markets of promise, with particular concentration on the areas of cardiovascular, ophthalmology, orthopaedics, and wound closure. Ethicon, Inc., continued as the world leader in the wound closure field.

LIVE FOR LIFE®

Putting the Credo philosophy to work challenged the thousands of Company employees all over the world who embraced the concept of "people helping people." They became involved in hundreds of community and civic projects, many of which received financial support from the Company. The Company's contributions program had become a vital instrument in carrying out the Credo's mandate to "support good works and charities…and encourage civic improvement and better health education." Taking into account annual donations of cash, products and land, the JOHNSON & JOHNSON Family of Companies ranks among the top ten American businesses in giving within the United States, as a percentage of profits.

In an organization that prided itself on decentralization, the Credo philosophy remained a unifying force. LIVE FOR LIFE became one of the most effective of all Credo-inspired programs, with a unique and successful system for altering the lifestyles of JOHNSON & JOHNSON employees worldwide. LIVE FOR LIFE was the inspiration of Chairman James E. Burke, who began it in the late 1970s. Its goal was to improve the health of employees with programs aimed at smoking cessation, better nutrition, weight control, exercise, blood pressure control and stress management. Burke's ambitious goal was to offer the employees of the JOHNSON & JOHNSON Family of Companies the opportunity to be the healthiest in the world. He also saw a successful LIVE FOR LIFE program resulting in higher morale and lower health care costs. Many of the Company's more than 200 plant and office facilities had LIVE FOR LIFE programs in place by 1986, and in those locations employee participation averaged nearly sixty percent annually. The results were impressive:

In seven years' time there were one-third fewer employees smoking.

The number exercising regularly had doubled.

Over eighty percent participated in a Health Profile, a comprehensive personal health assessment.

The rise in employee health care costs was reduced by one-third.

Absenteeism was down eighteen percent.

Another goal for LIVE FOR LIFE was to someday market it to other companies as a highly effective worksite wellness program. That became a reality by 1986 with the establishment of a new marketing division for LIVE FOR LIFE.

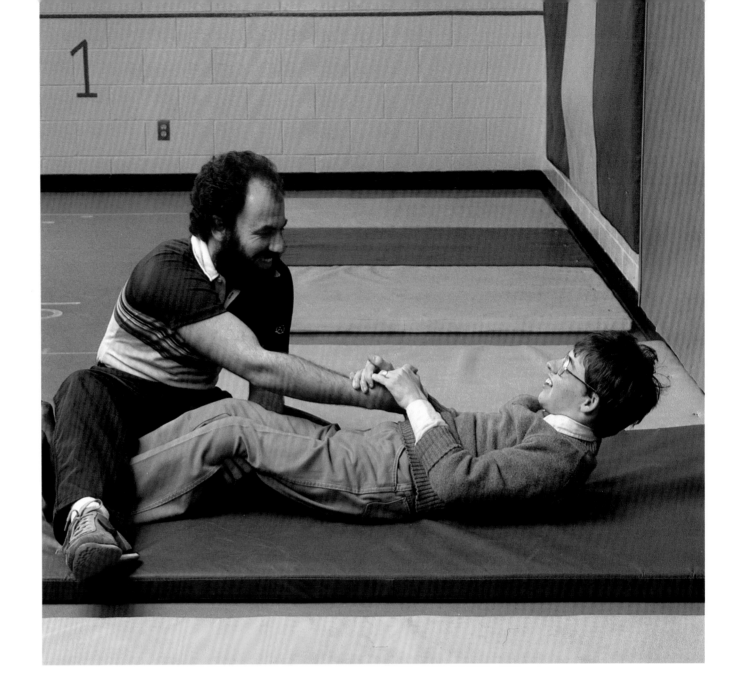

Dr. THOMAS N. GATES
MEDICAL DIRECTOR
McNEIL CONSUMER PRODUCTS CO.

In the fall of 1982, an unknown criminal used Extra-Strength TYLENOL Capsules as a murder weapon by adding cyanide poison to them, resulting in the deaths of seven people in the Chicago area. Overnight, TYLENOL toppled from its preeminent position as the nation's leading analgesic product and JOHNSON & JOHNSON and its McNeil Consumer Products Company were confronted with a crisis of nearly overwhelming proportions. It was a tragedy without precedent.

Within minutes of learning of the crime, the management of JOHNSON & JOHNSON took action to protect the public. This was accomplished by cooperating fully with the news media and with authorities in an all-out effort to warn and to keep the public informed, and by encouraging the prompt withdrawal of products when there was the slightest possibility of danger to consumers. Over time, TYLENOL capsules were with-

drawn from stores and homes across the United States and they were destroyed — some thirty-one million in all.

The magnitude of the TYLENOL tragedy and its impact on the nation was frightening. For the first time, people realized the potential for having an act of terrorism reach into the home. Suddenly, everyone became vulnerable.

In the days that followed, countless decisions were made by hundreds of people throughout the JOHNSON & JOHNSON organization. They were made under intense pressure — often with only a few minutes for deliberation — and they were made with the welfare of the public as a primary concern. The tragic experience highlighted as never before the unique value of the JOHNSON & JOHNSON Credo in defining responsibilities to consumers, employees, communities and stockholders. Never before had the principles embodied in the Credo been so severely tested.

The TYLENOL story became front page on virtually every newspaper in the country, and hundreds of hours were devoted to television news coverage. Early in the crisis, the Company made the decision to grant newspaper interviews and to have its key executives appear on television to explain the Company's actions. Led by Chairman James E. Burke, various Company executives went before the TV cameras and reinforced JOHNSON & JOHNSON's credibility. The reaction on the part of the news media and the public was extremely positive. *The Washington Post* summed up the Company's performance in this way: "JOHNSON & JOHNSON has effectively demonstrated how a major business ought to handle a disaster."

The business loss to JOHNSON & JOHNSON was enormous, and to a smaller company it might have been fatal. Most marketing experts predicted that TYLENOL would never recover. But from the beginning, a strong resolve swept through the entire Family of Companies. Everyone was determined to bring TYLENOL back, to restore confidence in the product and in the good name of JOHNSON & JOHNSON and McNeil. A sense of pride welled up; it became a company-wide crusade. The TYLENOL comeback was a tribute to skillful marketing strategy, months of laborious effort, and the undaunted spirit of those who believed it could be done. Immediately following the crime, all

TYLENOL television advertising was withdrawn for a short time. Then the Company began working to retain the confidence of TYLENOL users. Consumers were offered a free exchange of TYLENOL tablets for the capsules they had on hand. This was followed by a brief television advertising campaign featuring Dr. Thomas N. Gates, which simply asked the public to "Trust Us."

The critical decision was then made to return TYLENOL capsules to the market in new triple safety sealed packaging to thwart tampering, the first of its kind. This packaging was developed and ready for the market in the remarkable time of six weeks. Its introduction came at a televised news conference that was beamed to thirty cities via satellite. The marketing strategy of the relaunch of TYLENOL capsules included an offer of a coupon worth $2.50, which essentially gave consumers a free bottle of TYLENOL capsules in the new safety sealed packaging.

Within one year, thanks to the intrinsic fairness of the public, TYLENOL was back to its former preeminent position in the market.

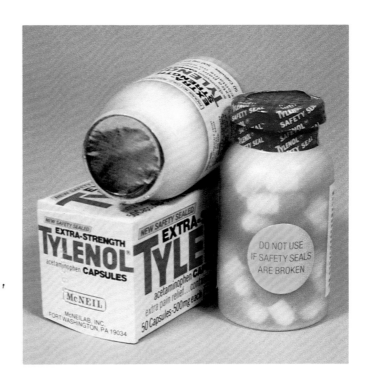

Maker of Tylenol Discontinuing All Over-Counter Drug Capsules

Offers to Replace Them After Woman's Death From Poisoned Pills

By ROBERT D. McFADDEN

Johnson & Johnson yesterday discontinued the manufacture and sale of all its over-the-counter medications in capsule form to prevent the kind of tampering that recently killed a woman who took cyanide-laced capsules of Extra-Strength Tylenol.

The company also offered, at its expense, to replace about 15 million packages of its capsule products in stores and homes across the nation with caplets, which are oval-shaped tablets coated to make them easier to swallow. It said it hoped to rebuild the lost capsule market in less tamper-prone caplets and tablets.

The phamaceutical concern, which markets scores of products and had sales of $6.4 billion last year, estimated that its withdrawal from capsules would cost $100 million to $150 million, after taxes. This will include the expenses of replacing six kinds of capsules already on the market and of retooling its plants as well as other costs in trying to rebuild its market position

'Standards of Responsibilit

"We feel the company ca guarantee the safety degree consistent standa

The New York Times / William E. Sauro

James E. Burke, chairman of Johnson & Johnson, at news conference with large model of oval-shaped tablet known as a caplet.

From JOHNSON & JOHNSON's perspective, the impossible happened in early February of 1986. There was a repeat of the TYLENOL contamination, this time in New York State, which resulted in one death from cyanide poisoning. Faced with another potential disaster, the Company again took swift action that closely paralleled what was done four years earlier. There was immediate and full cooperation with the news media, thereby alerting the public to any possible danger, and TYLENOL capsules were removed from store shelves in the area.

Within twenty-four hours JOHNSON & JOHNSON held a press conference — the first of three within a week — at its Corporate headquarters in New Brunswick. Company Chairman Burke, after expressing the Company's deep sympathy for the family of the victim, asked the public once again to place its trust in JOHNSON & JOHNSON and McNeil, as it had in 1982.

Events moved rapidly. When a second contaminated bottle of TYLENOL was discovered two days later, the Company issued a nationwide alert urging consumers not to use TYLENOL capsules. The decision was then made to discontinue the manufacture and sale of all over-the-counter medications in capsule form, because, as Burke said at a press conference: "We feel the Company can no longer guarantee the safety of capsules to a degree consistent with JOHNSON & JOHNSON's standards of responsibility to its consumers."

Burke then announced that the Company would replace at no cost all capsules in the hands of consumers and retailers, and urged

all users to convert to Extra-Strength TYLENOL Caplets, a new product in solid dosage form. Within a week the second TYLENOL tragedy began to turn around, and there was evidence of strong consumer support. On balance, the news media were again covering the TYLENOL crisis fairly, and became the Company's principal access to the public. Burke once again made numerous appearances on television, strengthening public confidence in the Company's actions and reinforcing the belief that JOHNSON & JOHNSON was a company that cared. Five months later the brand had firmly re-established its position as, by far, the leading pain reliever in America. JOHNSON & JOHNSON had not only

survived the two TYLENOL tragedies, but many felt that in the process it had become a much stronger company.

Before the first TYLENOL tragedy in 1982, JOHNSON & JOHNSON had been a company that preferred to keep a low profile. But that event, compounded by the repetition in 1986, catapulted JOHNSON & JOHNSON into a new level of public and media visibility, one from which it probably would never fully emerge. The Company found, however, that being the focus of more attention was easier to deal with when public confidence has been preserved.

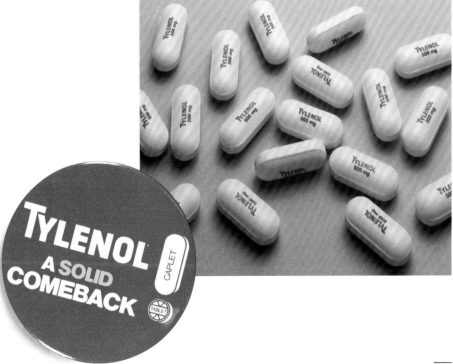

JAMES E. BURKE

ROBERT E. CAMPBELL

DAVID R. CLARE

DAVID E. COLLINS

CLIFTON C. GARVIN, JR.

JOHN J. HELDRICH

RALPH S. LARSEN

IRVING M. LONDON, M.D.

ARTHUR M. QUILTY

PAUL J. RIZZO

ROGER B. SMITH

HERBERT G. STOLZER

ANN DIBBLE COOK

JOAN GANZ COONEY

VICTOR J. DANKIS

ROBERT Q. MARSTON, M.D.

JOHN S. MAYO, Ph.D.

THOMAS S. MURPHY

JOHN C. WALCOTT

VERNE M. WILLAMAN

ROBERT N. WILSON

159

Abbruzze, Anthony J.	1971–1980
Anderson, Stanley C.	1970–1978
Boucher, Thomas O.	1959–1964
Burke, James E.	1965—
Campbell, Robert E.	1980—
Clare, David R.	1971—
Collins, David E.	1982—
Dankis, Victor J.	1976—
De Angeli, Frank	1972–1986
Dixson, Robert J.	1961–1972
Gibson, John J.	1968–1970
Haines, William J.	1969–1979
Heldrich, John J.	1977—
Hofmann, Philip B.	1955–1974
Holman, Wayne J., Jr.	1958–1973
Johnson, Robert W.	1955–1963
Johnson, Robert W., Jr.	1955–1965
Johnston, Donald D.	1975–1986
L'Hommedieu, Paige D.	1955–1961
Larsen, Ralph S.	1986—
Lienhard, Gustav O.	1955–1970
Lycan, William H.	1963–1969
McKenzie, Harry C.	1957–1963
Nelson, Wayne K.	1983–1985
Norman, Wilfred H.	1972–1975
Poole, H M, Jr.	1964–1971
Quilty, Arthur M.	1972—
Robinson, Vincent J.	1965–1971
Rohlfing, Anthony A.	1962–1967
Sellars, Richard B.	1957–1979
Smith, George F.	1955–1960
Smith, John J.	1967–1975
Smith, Norton L.	1955–1957
Stolzer, Herbert G.	1973—
Swank, Claude V.	1961–1968
Walcott, John C.	1980—
Whitlock, Foster B.	1964–1977
Willaman, Verne M.	1977—
Wilson, Robert N.	1983—

Our Credo

We believe our first responsibility is to the doctors, nurses and
patients, to mothers and all others who use our products and services.
In meeting their needs everything we do must be of high quality.
We must constantly strive to reduce our costs in order to
maintain reasonable prices.
Customers' orders must be serviced promptly and accurately.
Our suppliers and distributors must have an opportunity
to make a fair profit.

We are responsible to our employees, the men and women who
work with us throughout the world.
Everyone must be considered as an individual.
We must respect their dignity and recognize their merit.
They must have a sense of security in their jobs.
Compensation must be fair and adequate, and working conditions
clean, orderly and safe.
Employees must feel free to make suggestions and complaints.
There must be equal opportunity for employment, development and
advancement for those qualified.
We must provide competent management, and their actions
must be just and ethical.

We are responsible to the communities in which we live and work
and to the world community as well.
We must be good citizens — support good works and charities
and bear our fair share of taxes.
We must encourage civic improvements and better health and education.
We must maintain in good order the property we are privileged to use,
protecting the environment and natural resources.

Our final responsibility is to our stockholders.
Business must make a sound profit.
We must experiment with new ideas.
Research must be carried on, innovative programs
developed and mistakes paid for.
New equipment must be purchased, new facilities provided
and new products launched.
Reserves must be created to provide for adverse times.
When we operate according to these principles, the stockholders
should realize a fair return.

As we pause at this point in our history to look at our past, we see a remarkable record of growth…11.6 percent compounded over the last 100 years!

It is perhaps a propitious time to ask ourselves why JOHNSON & JOHNSON has outperformed the overwhelming majority of corporations so consistently, for so many years.

We are convinced the answer can be found in the basic philosophical convictions that have been shared by all previous managements since the corporation's inception. We have tried to capture those tenets in the statement:

"We believe the consistency of our overall performance as a corporation is due to our unique form of decentralized management, our adherence to the ethical principles embodied in our Credo, and our emphasis on managing the business for the long-term."

Even though our values remain constant, we are in many ways a very different company today as we respond to our rapidly changing world, and it is well to remind ourselves as we look to the next 100 years that how we shape the future is even more important than how we are rooted in the past.

It was clear to our management more than a decade ago that two major forces for change would create enormous new opportunities: first, an increasingly educated consumer getting more personally involved in managing his or her own health and, second, burgeoning new science and technology that would permit a revolution in the way we manage health care. We are now in the very early stages of that transformation. This Company is continuing the process of committing major investments in research and development as we challenge our managements everywhere to find more creative solutions for the myriad opportunities in the business of health care.

Health care is by its very nature a growth business, in that its goal is to satisfy a very legitimate yearning on the part of all mankind…the desire for a longer, healthier life.

As we look to the future, we are struck by the realization that we will not only be developing extraordinary new solutions to human needs, we will also be participating in redefining the very meaning of the words health care. How fortunate we are to be in a business that has as its mission

the prevention, diagnosis, and treatment of disease.
How truly wonderful it is that we have an infinite
number of pathways to pursue that mission, as well
as products that add to the consumer's well-being.

Our corporation is now well
organized to more effectively pursue these opportunities. We have a strong Board of Directors to help
challenge and guide us, and our growth will
be limited only by our individual creativity
and sense of purpose.

As long as we can continue to
attract and motivate the kind of talented and dedicated employees we have throughout our worldwide
Family of Companies, we have absolutely no
doubt the future will bring us even greater satisfaction
than our distinguished past.

JAMES E. BURKE
Chairman; Chief Executive Officer

DAVID R. CLARE
President; Chairman of the
Executive Committee

James E. Burke and David R. Clare

JOHNSON & JOHNSON
WORLDWIDE HEADQUARTERS
New Brunswick, New Jersey

Chicopee develops and manufactures products for use by other Johnson & Johnson affiliates, in addition to a wide variety of fabrics that are sold to a broad range of commercial and industrial customers. Chicopee's consumer products include disposable diapers for the private-label market segment.

Codman

Codman & Shurtleff, Inc. supplies hospitals and surgeons worldwide with a broad line of products including instruments, equipment, implants, surgical disposables, fiberoptic light sources and cables, surgical head lamps, surgical microscopes and electronic pain control stimulators and electrodes.

CRITIKON

Critikon, Inc. provides products used in the operating room and other critical care areas of the hospital. Intravenous catheters, infusion pumps and controllers, I.V. sets, filters and devices for monitoring blood pressure, cardiac output and oxygen are among its products.

evro

Edible natural protein sausage casings made by Devro companies in the United States, Canada, Scotland and Australia are used by food processors throughout the world to produce pure, uniform, high-quality sausages and meat snacks.

ETHICON

Ethicon, Inc. provides products for precise wound closure, including sutures, ligatures, mechanical wound closure instruments and related products. Ethicon makes its own surgical needles and provides thousands of needle-suture combinations to the surgeon.

Iolab Corporation manufactures intraocular lenses for implantation in the eye to replace the natural lens after cataract surgery, as well as instruments and other products used in ophthalmic microsurgery.

 JANSSEN
PHARMACEUTICA

Janssen Pharmaceutica Inc. facilitates availability in the U.S. of original research developments of Janssen Pharmaceutica N.V. of Belgium. Its products include SUFENTA, INNOVAR, SUBLIMAZE and INAPSINE, injectable products used in anesthesiology; NIZORAL and MONISTAT i.v. for systemic fungal pathogens; NIZORAL Cream 2% topical antifungal; VERMOX, an anthelmintic, and IMODIUM, an anti-diarrheal.

Johnson & Johnson
BABY PRODUCTS COMPANY

The Johnson & Johnson Baby Products Company produces the familiar line of consumer baby products, including powder, shampoo, oil, wash cloths, lotion and others. Additional products include educational materials and toys to aid in infant development, SUNDOWN Sunscreen and AFFINITY Shampoo and Conditioner.

Johnson & Johnson
CARDIOVASCULAR

Johnson & Johnson Cardiovascular manufactures and markets cardiovascular products used in open heart surgery that include HANCOCK Heart Valves, Vascular Grafts, MAXIMA Hollow Fiber Oxygenators, INTERSEPT Blood Filters and Cardiotomy Reservoirs.

Johnson & Johnson
DENTAL PRODUCTS COMPANY

The Dental Products Company serves dental practitioners throughout the world with an extensive line of orthodontic, preventive and restorative products. The company also provides dental laboratories with a broad line of crown and bridge materials, including the high-strength ceramic CERESTORE system.

Johnson & Johnson
HOSPITAL SERVICES

Johnson & Johnson Hospital Services Company develops and implements corporate marketing programs on behalf of Johnson & Johnson professional companies. These programs make it easier to do business with Johnson & Johnson and respond to the needs of hospitals, multihospital systems, alternative sites and distributors to reduce costs. Programs include Corporate Contracts and the COACT On-Line Procurement System.

Johnson & Johnson
ORTHOPAEDICS

Johnson & Johnson Orthopaedics markets innovative joint reconstruction products and fracture immoblization products.

Johnson & Johnson
PRODUCTS INC.

Johnson & Johnson Products' Health Care Division provides consumers with wound care and oral care products. The company also provides products to the athletic market.

McNeil Consumer Products Company

McNeil Consumer Products Company's line of TYLENOL acetaminophen products includes regular and extra-strength tablets, caplets and liquid; children's elixir, chewable tablets, drops and junior strength tablets. Other products include various forms of Co-TYLENOL Cold Formula, PEDIA CARE cough/cold preparations, SINE-AID, Maximum-Strength TYLENOL Sinus Medication, DELSYM cough relief medicine, and MEDIPREN ibuprofen pain reliever.

McNEIL PHARMACEUTICAL

McNeil Pharmaceutical provides the medical profession with prescription drugs, including analgesics, short and long-acting tranquilizers, an anti-inflammatory agent, a muscle relaxant and a digestive enzyme supplement.

Ortho Diagnostic Systems Inc. provides diagnostic systems for the clinical and research laboratory community. Products include instrument and reagent systems for the blood bank, coagulation and hematology laboratories as well as immunology systems and infectious disease testing kits.

Ortho Pharmaceutical Corporations's prescription products for family planning are oral contraceptives and diaphragms. Other products include vaginal anti-bacterial and anti-fungal agents. The Advanced Care Products Division markets non-prescription vaginal spermicides for fertility control, in-home pregnancy and blood sugar level test kits and an athlete's foot remedy. The Dermatological Division provides dermatologists with products for professional skin treatment.

Products for feminine hygiene—Stayfree Thin Maxi's, Maxi-Pads and Mini-Pads, Stayfree Silhouettes Body-Shape Maxi's, Assure & Natural Breathable Panty Liners, Carefree Panty Shields, Sure & Natural Maxishields, Modess Sanitary Napkins, 'o.b.' Tampons and related products—are the specialty of Personal Products Company. Other consumer products include Coets Cosmetic Squares, Take-Off make-up Remover Cloths and Shower To Shower Body Powder.

SURGIKOS

Surgikos, Inc. markets an extensive line of Barrier Disposable Surgical Packs and Gowns and surgical specialty products for use in major operative procedures. Other major products include Cidex Sterilizing and Disinfecting Solutions for medical equipment, customized sterile procedure trays for operating rooms, Surgine Face Masks and Head Coverings, Micro—Touch Latex Surgical Gloves and Neutralon Brown Surgical Gloves for sensitive skin.

Vistakon, Inc. develops, manufactures and distributes soft contact lenses. The company provides contact lens dispensing professionals with daily wear and extended wear lenses for nearsighted and farsighted persons. It also is a major supplier of specialty toric lenses for the correction of astigmatism.

XANAR Inc.

Xanar, Inc. specializes in products for laser surgery. Laser surgical devices can be used in general surgery and other surgical specialties to provide an effective, less invasive alternative to traditional techniques. Xanar's products include surgical lasers for gynecology, otolaryngology, dermatology and podiatry.

CHICOPEE

New Brunswick, New Jersey
Benson, North Carolina
East Camden, Arkansas
Gainesville, Georgia
North Little Rock, Arkansas
South Brunswick, New Jersey

CODMAN & SHURTLEFF, INC.

Randolph, Massachusetts
New Bedford, Massachusetts
Southbridge, Massachusetts

CRITIKON, INC.

Tampa, Florida
El Paso, Texas
San Jose, California
Southington, Connecticut
Vincentown, New Jersey

DEVRO, INC.

Somerville, New Jersey

ETHICON, INC.

Somerville, New Jersey
Albuquerque, New Mexico
Cincinnati, Ohio
Cornelia, Georgia
Chicago, Illinois
San Angelo, Texas

IOLAB CORPORATION

Covina, California
Claremont, California
Horsham, Pennsylvania
San Dimas, California
San Lorenzo, Puerto Rico

JANSSEN PHARMACEUTICA INC.

Piscataway, New Jersey

JOHNSON & JOHNSON BABY PRODUCTS COMPANY

Skillman, New Jersey
Royston, Georgia
Las Piedras, Puerto Rico

JOHNSON & JOHNSON CARDIOVASCULAR

King of Prussia, Pennsylvania
Anaheim, California

JOHNSON & JOHNSON DENTAL PRODUCTS COMPANY

East Windsor, New Jersey
Grand Rapids, Michigan
San Diego, California
Las Piedras, Puerto Rico

JOHNSON & JOHNSON DEVELOPMENT CORPORATION

New Brunswick, New Jersey

JOHNSON & JOHNSON FINANCE CORPORATION

New Brunswick, New Jersey

JOHNSON & JOHNSON HOSPITAL SERVICES

New Brunswick, New Jersey

JOHNSON & JOHNSON ORTHOPAEDICS

New Brunswick, New Jersey
Braintree, Massachusetts

JOHNSON & JOHNSON PRODUCTS, INC.

New Brunswick, New Jersey
Lemont, Illinois
North Brunswick, New Jersey
Sherman, Texas
Sun Valley, California
Gurabo, Puerto Rico
Las Piedras, Puerto Rico

MC NEIL CONSUMER PRODUCTS COMPANY

Fort Washington, Pennsylvania
Round Rock, Texas
Las Piedras, Puerto Rico

MC NEIL PHARMACEUTICAL

Spring House, Pennsylvania
Dorado, Puerto Rico

NORAMCO, INC.

New Brunswick, New Jersey
Athens, Georgia
Wilmington, Delaware

ORTHO DIAGNOSTIC SYSTEMS INC.

Raritan, New Jersey
Cambridge, Massachusetts
Carpinteria, California
Westwood, Massachusetts

ORTHO PHARMACEUTICAL CORPORATION

Raritan, New Jersey
Geneva, Illinois
Manati, Puerto Rico

PERSONAL PRODUCTS COMPANY

Milltown, New Jersey
Wilmington, Illinois

PHOTOMEDICA INC.

Raritan, New Jersey

SURGIKOS, INC.

Arlington, Texas
Clearwater, Florida
El Paso, Texas
Caguas, Puerto Rico

SYMEDIX

Wayne, Pennsylvania

VISTAKON, INC.

Jacksonville, Florida

WINDSOR MINERALS INC.

West Windsor, Vermont

XANAR, INC.

Colorado, Springs, Colorado
San Juan Capistrano, California

CANADA

Critikon Canada Inc.
Markham

Devro Canada Inc.
Markham

Ethicon Ltd.
Peterborough

Iolab Canada Inc.
Peterborough

Janssen Pharmaceutica Inc.
Mississauga

Johnson & Johnson
Baby Products Co.
Guelph

Johnson & Johnson Inc.
Montreal

McNeil Pharmaceutical
(Canada) Ltd.
Stouffville

Ortho Pharmaceutical
(Canada) Ltd.
Don Mills

Surgikos Canada Inc.
Peterborough

LATIN AMERICA

Argentina
Janssen Farmaceutica
S.A. C. e I.
Buenos Aires

Johnson & Johnson
de Argentina, S.A.
Buenos Aires

Brazil
Johnson & Johnson S.A.
Sao Paulo

Johnson & Johnson
Produtos Profissionais Ltda.
Sao Paulo

Chile
Johnson & Johnson
de Chile S.A.
Santiago

Colombia
Janssen Farmaceutica S.A.
Bogota

Johnson & Johnson
de Colombia S.A.
Cali

Costa Rica
Johnson & Johnson
de Costa Rica S.A.
Heredia

Dominican Republic
Johnson & Johnson
(Dominicana), C. por A.
Santo Domingo

Ecuador
Johnson & Johnson
del Ecuador S.A.
Guayaquil

Guatemala
Johnson & Johnson
Guatemala, S.A.
Ciudad de Guatemala

Jamaica
Johnson & Johnson
(Jamaica) Limited
Kingston

Mexico
Cilag de Mexico, S.A. de C.V.
Mexico City

Janssen Farmaceutica,
S.A. de C.V.
Mexico City

Johnson & Johnson
de Mexico S.A. de C.V.
Mexico City

O.D.S.
Mexicana S.A. de C.V.
Mexico City

Surgikos, S.A. de C.V.
Juarez

Panama
Ethnor del Istmo, S.A.
Panama City

Johnson & Johnson
Panama S.A.
Panama City

Peru
Johnson & Johnson
del Peru S.A.
Lima

Puerto Rico
Janssen, Inc.
Gurabo

Johnson & Johnson
Hemisferica S.A.
San Juan

Trinidad
Johnson & Johnson
(Trinidad) Ltd.
Trincity

Uruguay
Johnson & Johnson
de Uruguay S. A.
Montevideo

Venezuela
Johnson & Johnson
de Venezuela, S.A.
Caracas, Valencia

EUROPE

Austria
Cilag G.m.b.H.
Vienna

Janssen Pharmaceutica
G.m.b.H.
Vienna

Johnson & Johnson
G.m.b.H.
Salzburg

Belgium
Chicopee Coordination
Center N.V.
Brussels

Cilag N.V.
Herentals

Janssen Internationaal N.V.
Vosselaar

Janssen Pharmaceutica N.V.
Beerse

Ortho Diagnostic
Systems N.V.
Beerse

Denmark
Janssenpharma A/S
Birkerod

England
Codman Limited
Maidenhead

Critikon Limited
Ascot

Janssen Pharmaceutical
Limited
Grove

Johnson & Johnson
Cardiovascular Limited
Ascot

Johnson & Johnson
Limited
Slough

Johnson & Johnson
Orthopaedics Limited
London

Ortho-Cilag
Pharmaceutical Limited
High Wycombe

Ortho Diagnostic
Systems Limited
High Wycombe

France
Beghin-Say et
Johnson & Johnson
Paris

Cilag S.A.R.L.
Paris

Critikon S.A.
Paris

Ethnor S.A.
Paris

Johnson & Johnson S.A.
Paris

Johnson & Johnson
Cardiovascular S.A.
Paris

Laboratoires Janssen S.A.
Paris

Ortho Diagnostic
Systems S.A.
Aubervilliers

Surgikos S.A.R.L.
Paris

Germany
Cilag G.m.b.H.
Alsbach-Bergstrasse

Codman G.m.b.H.
Hamburg

Critikon G.m.b.H.
Norderstedt

Devro G.m.b.H.
Birkenfeld

Dr. Molter G.m.b.H.
Neckargemund

Ethicon G.m.b.H.
Norderstedt

Janssen G.m.b.H.
Rosellen

Johnson & Johnson
G.m.b.H.
Dusseldorf

Johnson & Johnson
Cardiovascular G.m.b.H.
Bad Homburg

Johnson & Johnson
Medical G.m.b.H.
Norderstedt

Ortho Diagnostic
Systems G.m.b.H.
Neckargemund

Greece
Janssen Pharmaceutica
S.A.C.I.
Athens

Johnson & Johnson
Hellas, S.A.
Athens

Ireland
Janssen Pharmaceutical
Limited
Cork

Johnson & Johnson
(Ireland) Limited
Tallaght

Italy
Cilag S.p.A.
Milan

Ethicon S.p.A.
Rome

Iolab S.p.A.
Rome

Janssen Farmaceutici S.p.A.
Rome

Johnson & Johnson S.p.A.
Rome

Ortho Diagnostic
Systems S.p.A.
Milan

Netherlands
Chicopee B.V.
Cuijk

Janssen Pharmaceutica B.V.
Goirle

JHC Nederland B.V.
Amersfoort

Johnson & Johnson
International Sales B.V.
Amersfoort

Johnson & Johnson
Medical B.V.
Amersfoort

Johnson & Johnson/Intradal B.V.
Amersfoort

Taxandria
Pharmaceutica B.V.
Goirle

Portugal
Janssen Farmaceutica
Portugal, Limitada
Lisbon

Johnson & Johnson
Limitada
Queluz

Scotland
Devro Limited
Moodiesburn

Ethicon Limited
Edinburgh

Surgikos Limited
Livingston

Spain
Janssen Farmaceutica S.A.
Madrid

Johnson & Johnson S.A.
Madrid

Sweden
Cilag Aktiebolag
Sollentuna

Janssen-Pharma AB
Helsingborg

Johnson & Johnson
AB
Sollentuna

Switzerland
Cilag AG
Schaffhausen

Cilag AG International
Zug

Cilag AG Products
Zug

Janssen Pharmaceutica AG
Baar

Johnson & Johnson AG
Spreitenbach

Turkey
Johnson and Johnson
Limited
Istanbul

AFRICA, ASIA and PACIFIC

Angola
Johnson & Johnson
(Angola) Limitada
Luanda

Australia
Cilag Pty. Ltd.
St. Leonards

Extal Pty. Ltd.
Westbury, Tasmania

Janssen Pharmaceutica
Pty. Ltd.
French's Forest

Johnson & Johnson
Australia Pty. Limited
Sydney

Johnson & Johnson
Medical Products Pty. Ltd.
North Ryde

Tasmanian Alkaloids
Pty. Ltd.
Westbury, Tasmania

China
Xian-Janssen
Pharmaceutical Ltd.
Xian, Shaanxi Province

Egypt
Johnson & Johnson
(Egypt) S.A.E.
Cairo

Fiji
Johnson & Johnson
(Fiji) Limited
Nasinu

Hong Kong
Johnson & Johnson
(Hong Kong) Ltd.
Hong Kong

India
Ethnor Limited
Bombay

Johnson & Johnson
Limited
Bombay

Indonesia
P.T. Johnson & Johnson
Indonesia
Jakarta

Ivory Coast
Johnson & Johnson
Cote D'Ivoire S.A.R.L.
Abidjan

Japan
Cilag Pharmaceutical K.K.
Tokyo

Janssen K.K.
Tokyo

Janssen-Kyowa Ltd.
Tokyo

Johnson & Johnson Japan Inc.
Tokyo

Johnson & Johnson K.K.
Tokyo

Johnson & Johnson
Medical K.K.
Tokyo

Ortho Diagnostic
Systems K.K.
Tokyo

Kenya
Johnson & Johnson
(Kenya) Limited
Nairobi

Korea
Cilag Korea Ltd.
Seoul

Janssen Korea, Ltd.
Seoul

Johnson & Johnson
Korea Ltd.
Seoul

Malaysia
Johnson & Johnson
SDN.BHD.
Petaling Jaya, Selangor

Morocco
Johnson & Johnson
Morocco S.A.
Casablanca

Mozambique
Johnson & Johnson
(Mozambique) Limitada
Maputo

New Zealand
Johnson & Johnson
(New Zealand) Limited
Auckland

Nigeria
Health Care Products
(Nigeria) Limited
Lagos

Pakistan
Johnson & Johnson
Pakistan (Private)
Limited
Karachi

Philippines
Janssen Pharmaceutica
Makati

Johnson & Johnson
(Philippines), Inc.
Makati

Singapore
Johnson & Johnson
Pte. Ltd.
Singapore

South Africa
Janssen Pharmaceutica
(Pty.) Limited
Randburg

Johnson & Johnson
(Pty.) Limited
East London

Johnson & Johnson
Professional Products
(Pty.) Ltd.
Halfway House

Taiwan
Johnson & Johnson
Taiwan Ltd.
Taipei

Thailand
Janssen Pharmaceutica
Limited
Bangkok

Johnson & Johnson
(Thailand) Limited
Bangkok

United Arab Emirates
Johnson & Johnson
(Middle East) Inc.
Dubai

Zambia
Johnson & Johnson
(Zambia) Limited
Ndola

Zimbabwe
Johnson & Johnson
(Private) Limited
Harare

SELECTED REFERENCES

Agreement, American National Red Cross-Johnson & Johnson, January 29, 1895.

Armour, Richard. DRUG STORE DAYS. New York. McGraw-Hill, 1959.

Chandler, Lester V. AMERICA'S GREATEST DEPRESSION, 1929-1941. New York. Harper & Row, 1971.

COLUMBIA ENCYCLOPEDIA

Cudd, John Michael. THE CHICOPEE MANUFACTURING COMPANY 1823-1915. Wilmington, Delaware. Scholarly Resources, Inc., 1974.

E. Mead Johnson's Mission, "Feeding Babies," MEDICAL TIMES, THE JOURNAL OF GENERAL PRACTICE. (The Men Who Made Medicine series), November, 1958.

"Edison and The Opera House Drug Store," AMERICAN DRUGGIST, December, 1931.

ENCYCLOPEDIA BRITTANICA

FACTORY MAGAZINE. October, 1966.

Freidel, Frank. AMERICA IN THE TWENTIETH CENTURY. New York. Alfred A. Knopf, Inc., 1960.

Hoehling, A.A. DISASTER — MAJOR AMERICAN CATASTROPHES. New York. Hawthorn Books, Inc., 1973.

Johnson & Johnson Annual Reports, 1944-1985.

Johnson, Robert W. "History of Plasters," THE PHARMACEUTICAL ERA, April 1, 1890.

Johnson, Robert W. OR FORFEIT FREEDOM. New York. Doubleday & Co., 1947.

Levathes, Louise. "The American Red Cross: A Century of Service," NATIONAL GEOGRAPHIC, June, 1981.

Morgan, H. Wayne. WILLIAM MCKINLEY AND HIS AMERICA. Syracuse, New York. Syracuse University Press, 1963.

NEW BRUNSWICK HOME NEWS. New Brunswick, New Jersey

Newman, Joseph, directing editor. 200 YEARS — A BICENTENNIAL ILLUSTRATED HISTORY OF THE UNITED STATES. Washington, D.C., U.S. News & World Report, 1973.

PHILADELPHIA INQUIRER, August 19, 1979.

PHILADELPHIA NORTH AMERICAN, June 22, 1918.

RED CROSS NOTES.

RED CROSS PRESS BOOK, 1882-1888.

"Robert Wood Johnson Talks It Over." Program 35 in the series.

THE NEW YORK TIMES.

THE RED CROSS MESSENGER.

The Johnson & Johnson Kilmer Museum, Reference Files.

THE SUNDAY TIMES. New Brunswick, New Jersey

PICTURE CREDITS

Copyright © 1941, 1975, 1986. by The New York Times Company. Reprinted by permission, pp. 104, 140, 156, 157.

The Bettmann Archive, pp. 50, 76, 96.

Barnes & Noble Books, Totowa, New Jersey. Reprinted by permission, p. 85.

Design:
Johnson & Simpson Graphic Designers
Newark, New Jersey

Major Still Life Photography:
Matthew Klein
New York, New York

Printing:
L.P. Thebault Company
Parsippany, New Jersey

Typesetting:
Arrow Typographers Inc.
Newark, New Jersey

Binding:
A. Horowitz & Sons
Fairfield, New Jersey

My associates have been very
generous in providing help with this book. Bob Kniffin
and Jim Murray reviewed the text and enhanced it with
their keen editorial judgment. Elisabeth King was a
persistent and accurate researcher, adept at locating photos
from the past. Over the years, I have repeatedly relied
on three very capable associates, Carol Dobrovolski,
Marian Lloyd and Terry McShane, and once again their
help was invaluable.

Robert Wood Johnson was still
Chairman of JOHNSON & JOHNSON when I first became
intrigued with him as an individual, and with the
colorful history of the Company. In those early forays into
the past Eunice McMurtry was most helpful, and some
of her efforts are reflected here. More recent but equally
competent research was done by a bright young graduate
student, Margaret Van Gluck.

To all of them, as well as to the many
others who responded with sound views on specific
subjects in the book, a very sincere thank you.

Finally, as designers, Milt Simpson
and Cathy Brennan-Walsh have an abundance of skills—
and patience—and I am grateful.

LAWRENCE G. FOSTER
Westfield, New Jersey
November 2, 1986

Cilag

CHICOPEE

Devro

Johnson&Johnson
BABY PRODUCTS COMPANY

ivlab

ETHICON

SURGIKOS

Johnson&Johnson
PRODUCTS INC.

McNEIL
McNeil Consumer Products Company

McNEIL
PHARMACEUTICAL

XANAR Inc

Ortho Diagnostic Systems Inc.